The Joy of
Being Catholic

The Joy of
Being Catholic

MITCH FINLEY

A Crossroad Book
The Crossroad Publishing Company
New York

1996

The Crossroad Publishing Company
370 Lexington Avenue, New York, NY 10017

Copyright © 1996 by Mitch Finley

Printed in the United States of America

Library of Congress Cataloging-in-Publication Data

Finley, Mitch.
    The Joy of Being Catholic / Mitch Finley.
        p.   cm.
    ISBN 0-8245-1551-X (hbk.)
    1. Catholic Church – Apologetic works. 2. Catholic Church – Popular
works.   I. Title.
BX1752.F56   1996
282–dc20   95-51421
                                                                CIP

*Technological society has succeeded
in multiplying the opportunities for pleasure,
but it has great difficulty in generating joy.*

—POPE PAUL VI,
On Christian Joy

Contents

Foreword

The book you hold in your hands does not pretend to offer a complete presentation of Roman Catholicism, its faith and traditions. This is not a catechism, and it is not a summary of Catholic doctrine. Rather, this book is an attempt to whistle up something of the spirit of Catholicism at its best. It's an appreciation and a celebration from the unique perspective of one particular Catholic writer. If someone else had written this book it would be a very different book.

If you want a more systematic and/or complete resource, but one still fun to read, the author recommends *The People's Catechism*, edited by Raymond A. Lucker et al. (Crossroad Publishing Co., 1995). If you want a more theological but still quite readable resource, get *Catholicism*, by Richard P. McBrien (HarperSanFrancisco, new edition, 1994). If you want the official Catholic resource, get *Catechism of the Catholic Church* (various publishers, 1994).

This book celebrates the spirit of Catholicism as a way of life, particularly its spirit of joy. This book is an act of love on the part of the author, an act of love for Roman Catholicism, its people, its institutions, and its centuries-old traditions. There are, no doubt, aspects of Catholicism that should be included in a book such as this one, but are not. There are advantages, however, to brevity.

The author finds being a Catholic a joyful affair of the heart, and he would share something of that joy with you. You are most warmly welcome.

What Is Catholic Joy?

Do you have a moment? I know you're busy; we're all busy. But can you spare a moment? Consider, if you will, for a twinkling, precious, golden, kind and gentle moment, the possibility — just the possibility, mind you — of ... joy. Imagine joy. Picture joy. Daydream joy. Let the possibility of joy as a way of life settle into your bones. For a moment, for one shining moment, imagine joy as the beginning, the middle, and the end of all that is, ever was, or ever will be.

What if your life were not pedestrian prose but a wonderful poem? What if your life were not a question but a revelation? Would this not be cause for joy? What if your life were not a sentence with a period at the end but a song that goes on and on? Would this not be cause for deep and abiding joy?

This, dear reader, is what Catholicism means by joy. Not that all Catholics find such joy in their faith at all times, in all places. A Catholic can fail to know the deepest truth of his or her faith as easily as anyone else. But I tell you, this is the heart of the Catholic matter, this joy, and those with a heart open to the truth, open to the Divine Mystery, will have this joy no matter what else may happen to them.

Catholics believe, quietly and in all humility, that Catholicism carries the deepest *potential* for Christian joy. In a world that thirsts for, chases after, and craves mere fun and mere thrills, Catholicism offers what is much deeper — joy. This joy does not depend on happenstance or chance. This joy does not depend on everything going my way. This joy is deeper than the deepest ✓ human anguish and more valuable than the best luck in the world. In the long run, the deepest tragedy cannot deprive us of this joy, and over the long haul the excitement of winning a twelve million dollar lottery is superficial by comparison.

A Catholic who does not understand what I say here has yet to grasp the full meaning of what it means to be a Catholic. If you, kind reader, are not a Catholic, do not be surprised to find that there are many Catholics who haven't a clue about the joy I talk about here. Do not be surprised; just take it in stride. There are, I dare say, a good many Christians of other theological inclinations who don't have a clue about what it means to be whatever they are, either. Many Jews, I dare say, don't have a clue about what it really means to be Jewish; many Muslims don't have a clue about what it means to believe in Islam. This is the way it is with us, who are well-meaning but spiritually challenged human beings.

None of this changes a thing. Catholic joy remains a possibility for those who care to make the little effort and take the great leap required to have such joy. At rock bottom, Catholic joy comes from faith, the believer's loving intimacy with God — the Divine Mystery, the Creator, the Ground of All Being, take your pick. Catholics have this joy because they experience, at the roots of their existence, loving intimacy with the God Jesus called his — and our — "*Abba*," an Aramaic term perhaps best translated as "Loving Papa."

Catholic joy comes, in part, from being able to relate to the Divine Mystery through an almost embarrassing wealth of metaphors, all of which are true, none of which ever say it all. God is Creator. God is Father or Loving Papa. God is Mother and the One who gives birth to us. God is Aroused Lover, and God is Compassionate Friend. Catholic poet Francis Thompson resorted to a canine metaphor, calling God "the Hound of Heaven," who pursues us "down the nights and down the days." And he was right.

Catholic joy comes from knowing that in the long run and the short run there is no need to be afraid or anxious because no matter what happens, good or bad, God's love for us is absolutely reliable, more trustworthy than the best things that can happen to us, more powerful than the worst things that can happen to us. Even death.

The joy that is Catholic is a joy that can happen any place and any time, and does. This is so because Catholic joy depends on nothing outside itself in order to be. It depends only on loving intimacy with God, and this loving intimacy can never be taken away from us. Never.

If you go looking for the stories, you will find Catholic joy in the most remarkable times and places and the most ordinary times and places. You will find Catholic joy in the most famous people and in the most obscure people. You will find Catholic joy in the Nazi death camps of World War II, and you will find Catholic joy in the most everyday homes and workplaces of here and now.

Maximilian Kolbe, a Polish Catholic priest and saint, died in Auschwitz in another man's place. According to witnesses, he did so with his face filled with joy. Stories like his, ancient and modern, are legion.

Linda and Michael, a Catholic married couple with no claim to fame, obscure as they can be, awoke one morning. The night before, they had gone to sleep worried and depressed. The bills were mounting up, Michael was unemployed, and they had four children under the age of eight. Linda and Michael lay in bed listening to their children play in the living room of their small rented house. They looked at each other, and for absolutely no reason they began to laugh with joy. Nothing had changed, but they felt joy in their many blessings. Stories like this, ancient and modern, are legion.

You will find Catholic joy at funerals because life goes on. You will find Catholic joy at weddings because life most definitely goes on. You will find joy among Catholics who have their doubts about institutional church issues; you will find joy among them because while they love the church's institutions, they don't substitute them for a loving God, whom they believe to be utterly unpredictable.

Are there Catholics who do not know Catholic joy? Of course, and such Catholics cause great mirth among the majority of other Catholics. You will not find joy among Catholics who take their religion too seriously. They are noisy, triumphalistic, and without humor. That is, they take their religion so seriously that they fail to see that joy is what it's all about. Such Catholics are a grim lot, indeed. Avoid them.

A Catholic journalist attended a conference put on by grim Catholics, and it was all she could do to get herself home again without going into a deep depression. If this is what being Catholic is about, she thought, no thank you very much. Fortunately, her faith does not depend on the behavior of a small minority of grim Catholics, so she recovered the true spirit of Catholic joy and went on.

Grim Catholics don't worship God. Grim conservative Catholics worship "official church teachings." Grim liberal Catholics worship the irrelevance of official church teachings. Both, for their own reasons, are convinced that the world is going to hell in a handbasket. Sin and corruption on all sides. No joy. As far as they are concerned, they are right and the rest of the world is wrong. What a burden they carry, the burden of being in possession of absolute truth, of having no doubts about anything. God help us.

Evelyn Waugh, a twentieth-century English Catholic, wrote a now familiar verse:

> Where e're the Catholic sun does shine
> There's music and laughter and good red wine.
> At least I've always found it so,
> *Benedicamus Domino!*

Waugh's words capture beautifully the spirit of Catholic joy. Life, sometimes, can be stressful. All the pressures, all the troubles, all the worries and anxieties. It's true, Catholicism says, all these things are real and difficult. Coping can be worrisome. Ah, well...all the same, let's have a party! "Music and laughter and good red wine!" The sun will go down, and we will die one day. Let's celebrate life!

Lent, the season of fasting, darkness, and repentance, begins tomorrow, Ash Wednesday. But Lent isn't here yet. Fat Tuesday! Mardi Gras! Costumes! Music! Dancing! Parades! Rejoicing!

You will find Catholic joy in places filled with light and places filled with darkness. Catholicism looks into the face of human suffering and tragedy, acknowledges it, and then digs deeper looking for the joy that must be hidden here someplace, if only on the other side. Catholicism looks into the face of human rejoicing and knows Who to be grateful to.

Catholic joy is not an escape mechanism, an easy out. It's the experience of meaning even in the midst of the greatest meaninglessness; the knowledge, even in the deepest darkness, that the light will return. As Catholic singer and song writer John Stewart wrote in one of his songs, "You can survive the darkest night / Remembering the sun." Catholic joy is possible because we believe that life is, indeed, a song that goes on and on. God is the singer, and we are the song.

This book is about various ways Catholicism can be a source of joy. It is an extended reflection on what a joy it can be to be Catholic. Such a book must be incomplete, of course, because there is no end to the joy of being Catholic. The author will be content if these pages inspire you, dear reader, to become more aware of the gift of joy in your own life.

CHAPTER ONE

The Joy of the Sacraments

Imagine, if you will. Let your imagination take flight. Pretend that you meet a friend you have not seen or heard from for a long time. You are delighted to see each other again. You embrace or shake hands. You smile. You laugh. Ah, your heart is touched. You talk, you bring each other up-to-date. Perhaps, with your old friend, there are tears of joy.

Now imagine that you meet this same friend and do nothing except look at each other. No embrace. No shaking hands. No smile. No laughing, no talking. No tears of joy. This would be a weird encounter, would it not? Unnatural, you might say, unnatural as can be.

What makes meeting an old friend a rich experience, a lovely, life-affirming experience, is the ways we demonstrate our affection for each other — the embrace, the shaking of hands, the smiling, laughing, and talking. The tears. Why is this so? Because by these actions we *feel* our friendship, we make it real, something from the heart that touches the soul.

We can't let our friendship remain inside us, unexpressed; we have to let it out, give it some fresh air. We are compelled to externalize it, and by doing this we renew our friendship and nourish it, give it a new lease on life. Only when we do this do we experience the joy of being with our friend again. The truth is — and it is a mystery — that when we do these things we are more alive than we were the moment before we met our old friend. We are both more alive than we were before. More alive. Imagine that.

Now put all this in the context of Christian faith, of loving intimacy with the Divine Mystery we call God. The sacraments Catholics cherish are special ways to renew and nourish our loving intimacy with the risen Christ. Because we are bodily beings — "embodied spirits," the great theologian Karl Rahner said — we crave ways we can lay our hands on to relate to spiritual realities. Therefore, we have the sacraments, visible carriers of an invisible reality — God's unconditional love for us. They are the hugs, the words, and the tears of the faith community's encounter with our dearest Friend.

A pale comparison: Just as our embrace of an old friend renews and nourishes our friendship, so the sacraments we can lay our hands on renew and nourish our loving intimacy with the risen Jesus. We can't let our friendship with Christ remain inside us; we have to let it out. That's what a sacrament is, and each one is more a poem than a mere handshake. Each one is more a dance than a simple embrace. You will see what I mean...

Catholics have seven sacramental rituals they lay their hands on: Baptism, Confirmation, Eucharist, Reconciliation, Marriage, Holy Orders, and Anointing of the Sick. We will discuss the special joy of each of these sacraments presently, but first something more basic, more down to brass tacks...

Scatter the brass tacks across the floor and read them, read them like runes. Here is what we read, that Catholics find joy in the sacraments because all of God's Creation is a sacrament, a carrier and giver of the Creator's love. That perplexing, driven, mind-blowing old tent-maker and genius, Paul of Tarsus, said it as well as any and far better than most: "Ever since the creation of the world [God's] eternal power and divine nature, invisible though they are, have been understood and seen through the things he has made" (Rom. 1:20).

Imagine that.

For the faith-filled heart, the vast and starry universe shouts and whispers that God is love. For the faith-filled heart, the heart on intimate terms with the Creator, the bursting, teeming earth shouts and whispers the fifteen-hundred-year-old words of St. Augustine of Hippo, that God is closer to us than we are to ourselves. All of Creation is in God, and God is in all of Creation. Tip-toe through the theological tulips, don't step on any of them, don't break a fragile stem or crush a brightly colored flower. See that the Creator is everywhere, but Creation is not God. Everything is in God, but God transcends Creation. See this and have joy, Catholicism says.

Listen. This is a truth as vast and endless as all of outer space. It is a truth as tiny as the smallest microorganism. Because all of Creation is in God, any part of Creation can be an occasion of God's loving presence. Feel God's presence as you gaze into an electron microscope at darting, wriggling beings so tiny they have dimensions smaller than the wavelengths of visible light. Bake a loaf of bread and know God's presence. Cultivate a garden of roses — or cabbages and carrots — and know God's presence. See an elephant or a giant sequoia tree, be amazed at their size and tonnage, and know God's presence. In human intimacy, especially, know God's presence. And feel the joy.

When we stand in awe before Creation we are ready to grasp something of the mystery of the sacraments. When we gaze with awe upon Creation we are prepared to know how ordinary things can carry the Holy of Holies. When we stand in awe before Creation we are in a position to know why simple elements such as bread and wine, words and water, committed love and sexual pleasure, can be occasions of joy for Catholics, can bring joy because, in truth, they are occasions for a close encounter with the Divine Mystery present in the risen Son of God.

Are you perplexed? Are you fascinated? Patience is a virtue...

Catholics find joy in the sacraments. They find joy because each one of the seven enables us to feel the graceful presence of the risen Christ. Each one enables us to know, up close and personally, the One who is already present in ordinary, glorious human existence. There is no magic here. No mumbo-jumbo, no hocus-pocus. No. Sacraments are gifts we receive, holy human rituals that open up and reveal the sacred in our midst. It's as simple, and overwhelming, as that.

For Catholics, the First Sacrament, if you will, is Jesus of Nazareth who became, and is now, the risen and cosmic Lord of time, space, and all Creation. "For in him," Paul says, "the whole fullness of deity dwells bodily" (Col. 2:9). This is joy. Christ is *the* sacrament of the human encounter with the Divine Mystery. In him, God is present in as full a manner as it is possible for human beings to experience. This is what we mean when we use the metaphor "Son of God" to describe who Jesus is.

Here is joy. Listen carefully. Each of the seven official sacraments brings us an experience of the One Sacrament, Jesus the risen Christ and Lord of history. Astounding, is it not? Takes your breath away, does it not? Silent, wordless prayer may be the only adequate response...

Baptism

We take some water, ordinary tap water. We say a blessing over the water, yet the water is already holy because God created it. We say a blessing over the water, a blessing from the heart. A person bows over a baptismal font, bows low, an act of humility. Humility. Imagine that. The priest or deacon pours the holy water over the person's forehead and speaks the ancient, ancient words, baptizing him or her, as Matthew's Jesus directs, "in the name of the Father, and of the Son, and of the Holy Spirit" (28:19).

Sometimes Baptism is a whole-body thing, not just a forehead thing, in the style of the early Christians who knew what they were up to. The person descends into a pool of water in an attitude of prayer and is buried in the water three times, "in the name of the Father, and of the Son, and of the Holy Spirit." This symbolizes, and accomplishes, the person's death to all that is *not* worth living for and rebirth to all that *is* worth living for.

The newly baptized receives an anointing with blessed oil, as the sign of the cross is traced on the forehead. As priests, kings, and prophets of old were anointed with oil, so we anoint the neophyte Christian as priest, prophet, and king. Old, old words. Ancient notions. They evoke mysteries alien to our time and place, and this is good. Through thought, prayer, meditation, and conversation with others, the neophyte Christian may discover what these old, old words mean for him or her in particular. But for now there is simply the oil in the form of a cross on the forehead, the planting of the seed.

The newly baptized receives a lighted candle. What can it mean to receive a lighted candle except that faith, loving intimacy with the Divine Mystery, is the most reliable light in a world sometimes steeped in darkness? What a light to have. What darkness and what a light. How to understand such a mystery? No trouble accepting the joy it brings, however. No trouble accepting the joy.

Often and very often, we baptize our children as infants, promising to do our best to raise them in the ancient faith. Precedent for this seems to go back, back, back to at least the time of the earliest Christians, perhaps to Jesus himself. In three of the four Gospels, Jesus says, "Let the little children come to me, and do not stop them" (Matt. 19:14, Mark 10:14, Luke 18:16). Do not stop them. We give our children all the good things we can, so why not all the spiritual gifts we can as well?

The Eucharist

The sacramental ritual Catholics experience most frequently is the Eucharist, or Mass. Through this ritual, we come closest to the embrace shared by two old friends, but it's more than that. It is far more than that. In the Mass, Catholics worship God and listen to readings from ancient Scriptures and to a homily that, ideally, applies the readings to the glory and anguish of our everyday lives.

In the Eucharist, Catholics know the joy of prayerfully sharing bread and wine that carry and cause the sacred presence of the risen Christ. In traditional language, the bread and wine become the "body and blood" of the risen Christ. But be careful, be ready, and be steady. Note that "body and blood" is a Semitic phrase that means "the whole person." The *risen Christ* is present, in his whole risen person, in the eucharistic bread and wine. I say this, but the moment the words fly out of my fingers, into my keyboard, and onto the monitor screen, I tell you that we know little about what these words mean. Precious little.

There is a great mystery, a great revelation here, and a joyful one. Metaphors and analogies fly though the air like angels, flapping their wings furiously trying to communicate realities that go beyond the human intellect, way, way beyond. In the Eucharist we commune intimately with the risen Christ, his living person, whole and entire, he who is already truly present in the community gathered in his name.

Thomas Merton, in *Life and Holiness* (1963), said: "The most sanctifying action a Christian can perform is to receive Christ in the Eucharistic mystery, thus mystically participating in his death and resurrection, and becoming one with him in spirit and in truth." What does this mean? God knows. God help us. It means that the Jesus we know intimately in the Eucharist and in Holy Communion is the Jesus who has been transformed as we shall be transformed on the other side of dusty death. What does this mean? God knows...

We know too, but as two lovers know each other, not as we know that a certain blend of hydrogen and oxygen makes water. Explain to me your love for one you love, and I will explain the Mass to you. The Eucharist is a mystery of God's unconditional love, God's passionate desire to be closer to us than we are to ourselves, and it is a cause for joy. The Mass is a revelation of divine love, and through the sharing of the whole person of the risen Christ those who share it come to know one another in a new light, in the light of God's love. And this is deep-down joy. Day in, day out, this is joy.

Some people see God in a beautiful sunset but deny the possibility that the transcendent Lord could be in bread and wine. Some people declare that God is everywhere, but have problems with the idea that the living Lord is present in bread and wine. If everywhere, why not in a particular place? If God is everywhere, what's the problem with the risen Christ, the Son of God, being present in bread and wine? Sometimes the human mind is too small to deal with how close God comes to us in Jesus and in the sacraments.

The Eucharist is the sacrament of God's love present in the weave of everyday life, if you will. Catholics participate in the liturgy of the Mass, at the very least on Sundays or Saturday evenings, but people celebrate the Mass daily, day after day, in countless parish churches that dot our cities and towns like so many punctuation marks in the stories of our lives.

Confirmation

Here is the truth, here are the facts. It won't take long to lay them on the table. The holy sacrament of Confirmation is a puzzlement. I can't tell you how much anguish has gone into trying to figure out the sacrament of Confirmation since the mid-1960s. Rite of adulthood? For a long time, most agreed that it was. A Catholic bar mitzvah. But no longer. That interpretation doesn't seem faithful to the sacrament's origins, long, long ago. In Confirmation the person receives, you might say, the fullness of the Holy Spirit. But what does this mean? God knows.

Catholics in some places give the sacrament of Confirmation at the same time as the child receives Holy Communion for the first time. Usually, at about the age of seven. Eastern Orthodox Christians confirm at Baptism. So who knows? It's a sacramental conundrum, but a joyful one. Maybe in a secondary sense the sacrament of Confirmation exists to remind us that we should not act like we have it all under control, that we know absolutely *everything* about everything, sacraments-wise.

Confirmation is a homely stepchild of a sacrament, it's true. Might as well confess. It's a one-time event to deepen the effects of Baptism and strengthen the person's bond with the entire community of faith. Anointing with oil, blessings and more blessings, and they add to the joy of being Catholic. Hey, why not?

Reconciliation

Being Catholic can be not only joyful but hilarious. For decades now, since the Second Vatican Council in the mid-1960s, Catholics of a certain age can't talk about being Catholic without speaking in two tenses at once. Here is how it *was,* here is how it *is.* Sometimes this gets hilarious. Prior to the late 1960s, we had a sacrament called Penance. Only everyone called it Confession. Today, the official name is Reconciliation, but many people still call it Confession. Like I said, hilarious. No problem. The purpose is the same.

At times, everyone acts in ways that are low down. We hurt other people. We lie, we steal, we cheat. We're mean. And later we hate ourselves for it. In our heart of hearts, we know we "done somebody wrong." Most of the wrong things we do, the bad choices we make, are merely selfish, prompted by anxiety, fear, or false pride. Now and then, of course, we do something that's bad big-time. We break an important promise, say. Or we let the desire for money get us by the throat so we neglect more important things in life.

Anyway, time marches on, and we know it's important to make it up not only with the person or persons we hurt or whose rights we violated. We also need to ask forgiveness of the God who gave us the freedom that allowed us to do what we did, the freedom we misused. *Mea culpa,* say the old Latin words, through my own darn fault. What a fool I am. God, I can't believe I did that. But I did.

Of course, we ask God's forgiveness and we believe that in that very moment, faster than the blink of an eye, our Creator forgives us. Just like that. All the same, we are fragile, fearfully made beings. You know. To sin, as we have, is a serious matter indeed. Sometimes just keeping it private, "between God and me," doesn't do the trick. The joy is not quite there, the joy of knowing forgiveness, of being reconciled heart and soul. This is what the sacrament of Reconciliation is for. To increase the joy. You can call it Confession if you want to; nobody cares.

Confession is good for the soul; even common wisdom tells us this. To sit down with, or kneel in a posture of humility before, a priest, one delegated by the church, and 'fess up, in general and/or in particular — this can be one of life's greatest joys. It's a very particular kind of Catholic joy. Strange as it may sound, it is a joy. It's a blessing not to be matched by anything you will ever feel on a psychiatrist's couch.

Marriage

Here is a sacrament to knock your socks off. A woman and a man fall in love, and the love they fall into, and deliberately choose to accept with both eyes open, is — are you ready for this? — the Divine Mystery itself. God. That's right. A man and woman "fall into" God when they "fall" in love. Or at least they find themselves in communion with the Divine Mystery in a way they had not experienced before. They were always "in God," of course, simply by the fact that they existed, were breathing in and out, walking around, laughing and crying, here and there. But when they fall in love with each other and make a relatively mature choice to accept each other in that love...well, that's something special.

If Christ is the sacrament of the human encounter with God, marriage is a special sacrament of the encounter with Christ. It's unique because this sacrament — this way we lay our hands on that is an encounter with the divine — is so human, so very, very human.

The "matter" of the sacrament of marriage is the love between a man and a woman, the laughing and crying, ecstatic and painful love that commits itself to lifelongness not just with a promise but with a vow. This committed, never-say-die love that we call marriage is a mystery, that is, an ongoing revelation of God's love.

Marriage is the only one of the seven sacraments where the one who officiates stands on the sidelines, acting merely as a witness for the community of faith on the wedding day. Bride and groom "administer" the sacrament to each other. Or rather, they crack the bottle of champagne on the bow of this sacrament called marriage that will sail on and on for as long as they both shall live.

Here is a secret so wonderful that I want to whisper it. Come closer. In their love for each other, husband and wife, wife and husband, experience the very love of God fully present in Jesus Christ, the Lord of history, of time and space and all Creation. Does this not tickle you? Think about it. Your average, run-of-the-mill, ordinary Catholic marriage is loaded with the loving presence of the Divine Mystery, the Creator of the universe. Can this be? Truly? Yes! This is what we mean when we say that marriage is a sacrament. Almost too much to handle.

More. Get a grip. Basic to the love shared by wife and husband is...sexual attraction. In the beginning and all down the line. God's love is in the sexual love shared by a married couple. When spouses make sexual whoopie, now and again they make babies and that is a knock-me-out glorious mystery. God knows.

But most of the time, when husband and wife make love, give each other intense sexual pleasure, the main purpose and effect is to nourish their love for each other. And when they nourish their love for each other they nourish their union in love with God in Christ. Therefore, sex in marriage is holy, and the deeper the pleasure the greater the holiness. That's powerful stuff there, my friend. Overwhelming as God's love is overwhelming. How's that for Catholic joy?

Of course, every coin has two sides, and here is the other side of the coin. Marriage has its downs as well as its ups. But even the downs of marriage are part of the ongoing sacrament the couple shares day-in, day-out. Husband and wife encounter God's love in the painful times, too, and when they are faithful to their commitment to each other, to the vows they make on their wedding day, on the other side of the growing pains they find an even deeper joy, a joy not to be described. This is God's own truth.

Holy Orders

We have the need for someone to call the meeting to order. The priest is the one who, in various ways, calls a local community of faith to order. We have the need for someone to represent a local community of faith, gather the community, listen to and wisely guide us. Called from among us, the priest is this person, and the sacrament that sends the priest into our midst is Holy Orders.

Holy Orders is for the priest an ongoing experience of the risen Lord. But in the priest the rest of us as well find the potential for encounters with Christ. The priest "administers" five of the other six sacraments (excluding marriage), but that is a bureaucratic-sounding word. "Ministers" the sacraments is better, but still inadequate. In ways unique to each one, the priest is meant to become a person who "enables" or "facilitates" the sacraments in ways that help them to be true encounters with the spirit of the risen Christ. In this sense, *who* the priest *is* becomes more important than *what* the priest *does*.

A priest is one of us first of all, a fellow member of the Christian community. Baptism says more about what a priest is than does the sacrament of Holy Orders. Even Pope John Paul II, in *Crossing the Threshold of Hope* (Knopf, 1994), declared that "*christianus* [Christian] has far more significance than *episcopus* [bishop], even if the subject is the Bishop of Rome."

Listen, now. This is important. We need priests, but where would priests be without the rest of us? No joy then. They are called from among us to be among us. A priest is a servant of the servants of God. Nothing is more disappointing or dispiriting to a community of faith than a priest who is on an authority trip or an ego trip.

There is great joy, however — great joy, I say — in a community where the priest is deeply, deeply in love with the Gospel, the Good News of God's unconditional love for us and for all of Creation. There is great joy when a local community of faith has a priest who knows that to be a priest is not to be an administrator or financial planner, who leaves such necessary stuff to others.

There is great joy when a priest knows that a good priest, a priest who cultivates joy, is not supposed to be an ecclesiastical legalist, cracking the moral whip over the heads of the people.

There is great joy when the priest is what a priest is meant to be: a humble spiritual leader and guide, one who brings healing and forgiveness and listens more than lectures. There is great joy in this, and so much potential for this joy.

Anointing of the Sick

In a frequently overlooked New Testament document called the Letter of James there is a passage that touches the heart. It touches the heart because it carries the true spirit of Christian kindness and compassion. Attend to it, please:

> Are any among you sick? They should call for the elders of the church and have them pray over them, anointing them with oil in the name of the Lord. The prayer of faith will save the sick, and the Lord will raise them up; and anyone who has committed sins will be forgiven. (5:14–15)

Read through the Gospels, up and down, slowly, quietly. You will find story upon story of Jesus healing those who are sick or afflicted. Story after story tells of the compassion and healing Jesus brought. And inevitably he leaves joy in his wake. This is what the sacrament of Anointing is for, to bring this same healing, compassion and healing, to those who need it.

It's a simple matter. People who are not well, seriously or not so seriously, in body, mind, or spirit, ask for the Anointing of the Sick. The priest anoints the person on the forehead with blessed oil, with the sign of the cross in blessed oil on the forehead. Prayers for healing and forgiveness provide the context and cultivate the spirit. And there is always healing of one kind or another. Always. This sacrament never fails to leave joy in its wake, joy of one kind or another.

CHAPTER TWO

The Joy of the Scriptures

This may astonish you, but here goes: Words can open up dimensions of the sacred. To say it another way, words can be sacramental. Words can be spoken or written carriers of an invisible reality, even the Divine Mystery we call, for lack of a better word, "God."

Amazing. Catholics gather much joy from the words in the Bible precisely because they are a kind of sacrament, a carrier of meanings and realities beyond the words themselves. For Catholics — and other nonfundamentalist Christians as well — the Bible is powerful because it is not an end in itself. The Bible is more like a prism through which "divine remarkables" can touch the human heart, mind, and soul.

To look into the Bible is not to face a concrete wall covered with words that mean what they say and say what they mean, and you had better pay attention lest God might get you when you least expect it. *Au contraire.* To look into the Bible is to gaze upon words written on clear glass, and when we gaze upon the words light filters through them from the other side of the glass, a light not of this earth.

Catholics do not worship the Bible; they worship the God they encounter there, a God of unconditional love, compassion, forgiveness, and... humor. Imagine a smiling God. The Bible includes more humor than we give it credit for. The trouble is we open the Bible and think, "Mm, gotta get serious here. This is *the Bible.* Serious stuff. Profound. Deep."

We open the Bible with preconceived notions, with a closed mind. We forget that Scripture is the Word of God in human words, and anything with a human element is bound to be funny sooner or later. Even the Bible.

The story of Adam and Eve in the garden of Eden has a tragic ending, but it's also a humorous story in a sad sort of way. We read it and smile, thinking how like us all. In his song "Dead Snakes," John Stewart sings: "The snake said to Eve, 'Come here, baby, / Bite my apple, it'll turn you to a lady.' / Eve took a bite and things got rough. / You can always get some, but you can never get enough."

The story of Abraham and Sarah is a funny story, too. Imagine God founding a new people through a couple of old crocks. Abraham is no fool, and he thinks it's hilarious. See: "Then Abraham fell on his face and laughed, and said to himself, 'Can a child be born to a man who is a hundred years old? Can Sarah, who is ninety years old, bear a child?'" (Gen. 17:17).

Abraham knew a knee-slapper when he heard one. It's very funny how God deals with His people sometimes, and the Bible never tries to hide this. There is joy in the pages of the Bible, and Catholics find it there. It's one of the joys of being Catholic.

For Catholics, the Bible is a source of joy because we know that it did not drop down out of heaven. Many writers put pen to papyrus, as it were, to produce the many kinds of writing that make up the Bible. All of them, to a one, were wild and crazy characters. They had to be wild and crazy to be able to write this stuff! We forget their humanity, I fear. We put a halo above their heads, place them on a pedestal, and turn them into unreal note takers.

What a shame. Perhaps the people who wrote the Bible were a lot like you and me, fairly average people who had a thing about writing, that's all. And when their faith — their personal experience of God's love — compelled them to write, they wrote. Writers are like that, you know. They can't help but write about just about anything. Something good happens, they write about it. Something bad happens, they write about it. Something ordinary happens, they have a tough time not writing about it.

That's why the Scriptures bring joy, because they come from the religious experience of ordinary people. We can identify with what we find in the Bible if we resist the inclination to hold it at arm's length, thinking it's too holy for the likes of us. This is the Catholic way, to grab the Bible with both hands, open it, throw caution to the winds, and jump in. Catholics feel a need to wrestle with the Scriptures, sometimes even grab the scriptural Word of God and give it a good shake, saying, "Come on, deliver!"

"But, but, but, but-but, ..." you may say. Isn't the Bible the inspired Word of God, free from all error and what have you? Yes. And no. Catholics believe — here comes more joy — that God used the very human talents and abilities of a slew of writers over many centuries to produce the biblical documents. Catholics do not believe that the Holy Spirit sat down at an executive desk one day, called in a human person, and said, "Take dictation, please. Ho hum, time to write another part of the Bible."

Catholics rejoice that the Scriptures came into existence by means of human, historical processes not unlike the ones that produced the writings of Plato or Shakespeare. The big difference is that the human experiences that led to the writing of the biblical documents were a faith community's experiences of the Divine Mystery. The experiences that led Bill Shakespeare to write *Hamlet* were his own. Also, the Bible's explicit purpose is to nourish faith, whereas Shakespeare's purpose is to entertain and touch the human heart by means of dramatic presentation. The Bible is the Word of God. *Hamlet* is the word of Shakespeare.

There is Catholic joy in the conviction that the Bible is free from error whenever it touches on anything having to do with our experience of spiritual healing and liberation (salvation). Don't expect free-from-error in the Bible, however, when it comes to historical facts, biology, cosmology, psychology, and the like. The Bible is not a science text or a history text. Thank God. Remember, we're talking about documents written in times, places, and cultures far, far away.

There is joy in the Catholic conviction that the Bible includes many different literary styles, from historical narrative to poetry, from a unique literary form called "Gospel" to letters and fantasies. One book, the Song of Songs, is a poetic celebration of human erotic love. Eroticism in the Bible! Whoa. There is joy in learning how each literary style works in order to convey God's own truth.

No need to read the Book of Revelation anguishing over when the end of the world will happen. The author of Revelation noodled around and came up with this particular fantastic literary style as a way to inspire hope, not fear.

No need to develop a permanently furrowed brow from puzzling over chapter 13 of Mark's Gospel, trying to figure out when Jesus will return. Predicting the future is not what it's about. Joy and hope are what it's about. There is joy in leaving the future to a loving God who seems to Catholics to be more interested in beginnings than endings, more interested in peace and joy than worry and fear.

There is joy in the Scriptures, great joy. Not on every page, of course. Certain documents in the Old Testament have their share of blood and gore, wars, brutality, and sexual high jinks. Even when we read about such, however, if we keep reading we see that God brings joy out of sorrow. As far as Catholics are concerned, by and large when you talk about the Bible you talk about a wisdom that leads to joy.

There is a joyful unity, for Catholics, between the Old and New Testaments. Jewish readers see the documents we call "Old Testament" in the light of their own faith and traditions. Catholics and other Christians read these documents in the light of their experience of Jesus as the Messiah and Son of God. Thus, for Catholics the New Testament sheds light on the Old Testament and vice versa. There is joy in this because it gives us a feel for our roots, where we came from as a people.

The Gospel of Matthew has an especially strong interest in understanding Jesus as the fulfillment of Judaism's ancient hopes for a Messiah. Right at the start, Matthew reels off a long list of names of people who, theologically at least, constitute Jesus' family tree. Read it clear through if you want to, but it's not necessary. You might want to just skim the text to get the basic drift:

An account of the genealogy of Jesus the Messiah, the son of David, the son of Abraham. Abraham was the father of Isaac, and Isaac the father of Jacob, and Jacob the father of Judah and his brothers, and Judah the father of Perez and Zerah by Tamar, and Perez the father of Hezron, and Hezron the father of Aram, and Aram the father of Aminadab, and Aminadab the father of Nahshon, and Nahshon the father of Salmon, and Salmon the father of Boaz by Rahab, and Boaz the father of Obed by Ruth, and Obed the father of Jesse, and Jesse the father of King David. And David was the father of Solomon by the wife of Uriah, and Solomon the father of Rehoboam, and Rehoboam the father of Abijah, and Abijah the father of Asaph, and Asaph the father of Jehoshaphat, and Jehoshaphat the father of Joram, and Joram the father of Uzziah, and Uzziah the father of Jotham, and Jotham the father of Ahaz, and Ahaz the father of Hezekiah, and Hezekiah the father of Manasseh, and Manasseh the father of Amos, and Amos the father of Josiah, and Josiah the father of Jechoniah and his brothers, at the time of the deportation to Babylon. And after the deportation to Babylon: Jechoniah was the father of Salathiel, and Salathiel the father of Zerubbabel, and Zerubbabel the father of Abiud, and Abiud the father of Eliakim, and Eliakim the father of Azor, and Azor the father of Zadok, and Zadok the father of Achim, and Achim the father of Eliud, and Eliud the father of Eleazar, and Eleazar the father of Matthan, and Matthan the father of Jacob, and Jacob the father of Joseph the husband of Mary, of whom Jesus was born, who is called the Messiah. So all the generations from Abraham to David are fourteen generations; and from David to the deportation to Babylon, fourteen generations; and from the deportation to Babylon to the Messiah, fourteen generations.

(Matt. 1:1–17)

Matthew's genealogy does not make the most interesting reading in the world. In fact, it's a real snoozer. That's why this long quotation is in small print, so you can get the idea without having to read the whole thing. The point is to see how important it was to Matthew to show that Jesus had (theological if not literal) family connections that went way back to the origins of the covenant between God and Abraham. Matthew wanted his first readers — many of whom were Jewish converts to Christianity — to gather joy from seeing that the Jesus in whom they had placed

their faith did not separate them from their past but brought it
to fulfillment.

The human writers of the Gospels felt compelled to insist that
Christianity was the fulfillment of Judaism, even to the point
of implying that Judaism was now passé. It was probably necessary for them to do this to establish the church's identity as
a distinct community of faith. Today, however, Catholicism acknowledges and repents of its role in past persecutions of Jewish
people and rejects any suggestion of anti-Semitism. Instead, we
cherish Judaism, for the church cannot forget, in the words of the
Second Vatican Council, "that she draws nourishment from that
good olive tree onto which the wild olive branches of the Gen-
tiles have been grafted" (*Declaration on the Relation of the Church
to Non-Christian Religions*, no. 4; see Rom. 11:17–24).

One of the deepest sources of joy for Catholics comes from
the fact that Jesus taught by telling stories, and we have these
stories still, even if adapted for particular audiences for whom the
four Gospels were written. Pick up a copy of the New Testament.
Open to the Gospel of Luke, and flip the pages until you find
Jesus' familiar story about the Good Samaritan, in chapter 10.
Open the story, but open your heart as well, if you would know
the joy this story can bring.

Notice that Jesus tells the story of the Good Samaritan following an exchange of words with a lawyer who decided to put him
to the test. This lawyer is not the same as lawyers of our own
time and place. Scholars are not sure about the place of such a
lawyer in first-century Palestine, but he was an expert in the Mo-
saic law of Israel, almost certainly, and he was among those who
opposed Jesus.

The lawyer looks Jesus in the eye and shoots from the lip.
"Teacher," the lawyer says, "what must I do to inherit eternal
life?" Jesus, cool as can be, replies with a question of his own.
"What is written in the law? What do you read there?"

This is not what the lawyer expected. Still, he recovers nicely.
He knows his stuff, in his head if not in his heart. "You shall love
the Lord your God with all your heart, and with all your soul, and

with all your strength, and with all your mind; and your neighbor as yourself."

Exactly, Jesus says. Do this and you will have eternal life. But the lawyer will not be put off so easily. If he leaves the dialogue at this point it will look to witnesses like he failed to make any points against Jesus. So he smugly fires back: "And who is my neighbor?"

Good question. Very good question indeed. You might think that Jesus would give a well-phrased, concise definition of "neighbor." But no. For Jesus, love is not a matter of abstractions but of actions. So he tells a story. A story, come on over here and I will tell you a story. Great way to get the attention of the crowd as well.

Jesus tells the story of the Good Samaritan, the story we know so well, so very well. We know it so well we can tell it ourselves. We are so familiar with this story that . . . we have forgotten what it means. For us, the story of the Good Samaritan is a cliché. More's the pity.

In truth, the story of the Good Samaritan is a song for the soul. This story calls us to find each of the characters in ourselves. In myself I can find something of the "man going down from Jerusalem to Jericho," the robbers, the priest, the Levite, and the Samaritan.

It's unavoidable. Life kicks us around to one degree or another. We are all victims. But this is no invitation to self-pity. There is no room for whining or feeling sorry for myself. Everyone has hard times, and others have had a tougher time than I. Rather, there is joy in knowing that we have been cared for by others, the Good Samaritans in our life. When life knocked us around, there have been others there to listen, to care, to extend a hand. Think what life would have been like without the Good Samaritans who came along, who helped us when they could have passed on by. There is joy in this.

We find in ourselves too those who kept traveling, the priest and the Levite. They look and turn away. Like we do. There's a guy lying in the ditch, beaten up it looks like. Ick. Probably his own fault. What can I do? Ought to get a job and stop living such a life.

Man, woman, and child stand on the street corner as we drive by. Man holds a sign. "Homeless. Please help us eat today." We drive on. What can we do? Probably their own fault. Why don't they get jobs? Pass on by, pass on by, almost always we pass on by. What can we *do?* What can *we* do? *What* can we do?

It's all a mix, of course. We are not always so quick to pass by. Let's give ourselves credit where credit is due. Sometimes we are also the Good Samaritan, and there is joy in this. We do what we can when we can. We go out of our way; we inconvenience ourselves. We don't always pass the panhandler on the street who asks if we have any change. Sometimes we give him or her some change. We send donations to worthy causes. We give food to our local food bank. We help build a Habitat for Humanity house. We do what we can when we can. Like the Good Samaritan. We are a good neighbor.

But wait. Are we sometimes the robbers, as well, the bad guys, the ones who beat and abused and robbed an innocent traveler? Yes, we are. Like it or not, we sometimes are. Who do we abuse and rob? Think about it, think long and hard about it.

Do we approve when our government supports foreign dictatorships that torture and murder people for political reasons? Do we look the other way? Then we are guilty by our silence. Do we remain silent when our local city government refuses to do more for the homeless? Do we remain silent? Sometimes, at least, we do. We feel so overwhelmed already with life's responsibilities, and so we do nothing. By default, that makes us robbers and thieves, people who support people who neglect the neglected.

This should not be cause for beating ourselves up, of course. But we need to acknowledge the truth and see where it may lead us. Could be it will lead us in directions we would not take otherwise. Could be.

Then, of course, we have the Samaritan, the hero of the story. The idea of a "good" Samaritan was almost impossible for the lawyer to imagine. Samaritans, by definition, were the scum of the earth as far as the lawyer and his ilk were concerned. Here Jesus was saying that a Samaritan could be "good." The very idea! What nerve! But don't we do the same sometimes? Can we imagine a "good hypocrite"? A "good multinational corporation"?

Jesus' concluding message to the lawyer is, of course, his main message to us as well. "Go and do likewise." Do as the Samaritan did. There is joy in this directive, because it makes it quite simple to be a follower of Jesus. All we need do is "go and do likewise." Care for others, even if it costs you. We don't do it perfectly or always, but we do it. And there is joy in continuing to try, because this is the only way, the only way to have a life worth living.

The story of the Good Samaritan is loaded with joy because its message is so simple. Life is not a tough nut to crack, the story says. Life is a beautiful gift to open. Life is not a puzzlement; life is a revelation. Life is not difficult to figure out. It's quite simple. "Get a life," comes the derisive taunt. No problem. To "get a life" all we need do is look for ways to care for others that suit our talents best. What a joy.

The joy we find in the Bible is the joy that comes from knowing that life is a gift to be given away. How will I give my life away? That's the only question we must answer for ourselves. Not that this can be easy all of the time, of course. In fact, sometimes it can be difficult, even painful. Matthew's Jesus lays it on the line: "If any want to become my followers, let them deny themselves and take up their cross and follow me. For those who want to save their life will lose it, and those who lose their life for my sake will find it" (16:24–25).

You may say: You call this a joyful message? What kind of joy is this, anyway? This does not sound like joy. No way.

When Jesus talks like this, we squirm like worms. This does not sound like fun. All the same, there is joy in such sayings of Jesus. Stick around and you'll see what I mean. The key to finding the joy here is to understand the divine paradox.

Jesus says that in order to save my life I must lose it. This means that only if I forget myself will I find myself. Granted, this is difficult, losing oneself; it's like carrying a heavy cross sometimes. But the self we need to lose is a false self, an illusion. The self we must give up is the self that is selfish, self-centered, pre-occupied with self. The self we must ignore is the self the mass market advertising industry constantly urges us to coddle, bathe, protect, and pamper. The self we must lose is the self we worry about. What about me? What about me? That's the illusory self. When we forget or ignore this self in order to live for others, then we really live. Then we live, even now, the life that we call "eternal." Then we discover our true and deepest self. That's the point. And there is joy even in the struggle to do this. There is joy.

It's simple...and not so simple. Sometimes people reflect on this need to forget oneself and focus on others, and they leap-frog to the conclusion that they should avoid any action that looks like it might be self-centered. Wrong. There is joy in knowing that we need times to take care of ourselves if we want a healthy self to give away to others. I can't share new ideas with others unless I take time to read a book. I can't care for others unless I take time to care for myself. I need time to listen to good music. I need time for solitary, silent prayer and reflection. I need time for exercise, and I need good nutrition. I need to focus on myself sometimes but for unselfish reasons, in order to be able to focus on others.

There is joy, too, in learning to use the Scriptures for prayer. Catholic tradition calls one approach to scriptural prayer *lectio divina*, which we might translate as "holy reading." There is nothing esoteric about this, so don't get nervous. In fact, nothing could be simpler. *Lectio divina* is simply a way to let Scripture lead us into quiet, meditative, relaxing prayer. It doesn't take much time; that's entirely up to the one doing the praying.

Any book of the Bible is appropriate for *lectio divina*, but the Book of Psalms is an excellent selection to begin with. Here is a simple, ten-step approach:

1. Find a comfortable place to sit.

2. Sit there.

3. Open the Psalms at random. Say you come up with Psalm 5. Good.

4. Begin reading the first verse of Psalm 5. "Give ear to my words, O LORD; give heed to my sighing."

5. Maybe this first line gently grabs you. Maybe you are in some difficult space in your life right now, and you do your share of sighing.

6. Read the same line again. "Give ear to my words, O LORD; give heed to my sighing." Read the line again. It's short, so now you have no trouble reciting it silently with your eyes closed.

7. Say this same line over and over silently to yourself. Let the words settle into your heart. See where they lead you, maybe to other words of your own you want to say to the God who dwells in you. Speak about whatever makes you sigh these days.

8. Unburden yourself in words as long as you like. Then let yourself slip into a silent, loving presence before God. Just let yourself be there for as long as you wish.

9. When that time passes, open your eyes and keep reading the Psalm. When you come to another line that touches your heart, pause and go through the same quiet process again.

10. Let various lines lead you into various kinds of prayer — prayer of worship, prayer of petition, prayer of thanksgiving. That's *lectio divina*.

Simple, right? Remember, you can use any part of the Bible, almost, for this kind of prayer. Sometimes a saying of Jesus from one of the Gospels works well. Other times a line from one of St. Paul's letters will do. Regardless, read slowly through the text, pausing for silent prayer whenever you come upon a line that has special meaning for you at the moment. This is a Catholic form of prayer that can become a deep source of joy the longer you practice it.

The joy Catholics find in the Scriptures has many dimensions, and sometimes this joy comes in ways we would rather avoid. There is an old saying that the Gospel should comfort the afflicted and afflict the comfortable. We have no trouble with the first part, of course, and God knows we need all the comfort we can get sometimes. But when it comes to being challenged where we are most comfortable, that's another matter, an unwelcome twist.

There is joy in allowing the Gospel to drag us out of our self-complacency. Perhaps we are Catholics who sit each Sunday or Saturday evening in a beautiful church, perhaps a plush new parish church with soft, upholstered pews. Perhaps we listen to the Gospel reading for this Sunday, and it goes like this, Jesus speaking:

> "Blessed are the poor in spirit, for theirs is the kingdom of heaven. Blessed are those who mourn, for they will be comforted. Blessed are the meek, for they will inherit the earth. Blessed are those who hunger and thirst for righteousness, for they will be filled. Blessed are the merciful, for they will receive mercy. Blessed are the pure in heart, for they will see God. Blessed are the peacemakers, for they will be called children of God. Blessed are those who are persecuted for righteousness' sake, for theirs is the kingdom of heaven. Blessed are you when people revile you and persecute you and utter all kinds of evil against you falsely on my account.
>
> "Rejoice and be glad, for your reward is great in heaven, for in the same way they persecuted the prophets who were before you. You are the salt of the earth; but if salt has lost its taste, how can its saltiness be restored? It is no longer good for anything, but is thrown out and trampled under foot.
>
> "You are the light of the world. A city built on a hill cannot be hid. No one after lighting a lamp puts it under the

bushel basket, but on the lampstand, and it gives light to all in the house. In the same way, let your light shine before others, so that they may see your good works and give glory to your Father in heaven." (Matt. 5:3–16)

And perhaps the homily, following the readings from Scripture, is about the need for more money to pay for new carpet for the church, or new fixtures, or new this or that. Perhaps the homily sidesteps the Gospel, which is a great sadness that leaves us undisturbed in our faith.

We like to be undisturbed in our faith. Cozy. That's a faith we can live with. But if that is the faith we cultivate, it leaves us, to borrow words from songsmith Paul Simon, "empty as a pocket." Spiritually, humanly, empty as a pocket. No joy. Can we live with no joy as long as we are cozy? Many seem to prefer it...

Catholic joy finds its deepest depths in our souls when we give ourselves a shake, when we sit up and pay attention, when now and then we allow the Gospel to ring in our ears like a slap in the face. Then the possibilities for joy are almost endless, and cozy can't compare to genuine spiritual joy. No comparison whatsoever.

The Good News is that I am, and we all are, loved by God. No strings attached. No small print. No red tape. No hassles. Once we accept and really believe that God's love is trustworthy, in the long run and the short run, then we need no longer cling to the empties, the empties we grasp like your basic drowning man grabbing at straws afloat on the water's surface.

We can give up clinging to the empties, which include other people's opinions of us, financial forms of security as the ultimate form of security, possessions, affluence, the "inner child," and addictions of all kinds. The empties are legion, and while they seem reliable at first, in the end they are empty as an old tin can.

There is joy in responding to Jesus' quiet invitation to turn loose of the empties so there will be room for the Spirit of joy to come in. This is the heart of the Scriptures, the call to cast off the chains we bind ourselves with so Christ can give us true liberty of heart and soul. This is the meaning of Jesus' saying, his most basic message: "The time is fulfilled, and the kingdom of God has come near; repent, and believe in the good news" (Mark 1:15).

There is joy in that word "repent." Believe it or not. The Scriptures offer comfort, but they also prod us to grow up, stop whining, and get on with it. Live like the free person you are. Live as if you had faith and you will have faith. Live as if God were worthy of complete trust. You will find that it's true. That's what the Scriptures say, and therein we find tremendous joy.

One more thing, a mere by-the-by. In order to plumb the depths of the joy of being Catholic, we must make time to read — and read about — the Scriptures. Some Catholics don't know this joy because they hardly ever read the Bible on their own. The Scriptures echo in the distance at Sunday Mass, but that's about it. So, we've got to pick up the Bible and read it. Or rather, we've got to pick up the Bible and dive into it. And submerge ourselves in joy.

CHAPTER THREE

The Joy of Community

Poet T. S. Eliot (1888–1965) was a conjunction of contradictions. He was an American, born in St. Louis, Missouri, but he lived much of his life in England as an English banker. He also was not a Catholic — close, an Episcopalian — but his poetry is charged with the spirit of Catholicism.

In his poem "Choruses from 'The Rock,'" written in the 1920s, Eliot offered a most Catholic observation: "What life have you if you have not life together? / There is no life that is not in community, / And no community not lived in praise of God."

The Catholic Church is above all a community of faith. Where e're the Catholic sun does shine you'll find the joy of community. Actually, a clarification is in order. Community, the idea of people being together in a faith context to support and depend upon one another in various ways is as Catholic as it can be. But sometimes Catholic parish communities don't *seem* very communal. You can attend Mass in some Catholic parishes and get the feeling that everyone is there to worship God and the heck with my neighbor.

But Catholicism is and always has been big on community. Catholicism doesn't place solitary worship at the center of Catholic life. We worship together. We call the Mass, a communal activity, the "summit and source" of the church community's life. It all comes down to what you mean by community.

Is the only kind of faith community the kind where everyone is very extroverted, lots of glad-handing going on, whopping

43

folks on the back, yukking it up? Is the only kind of faith community the kind where you can't walk in the front door of the church on a Sunday morning without having an official greeter greet the daylights out of you? Is the only kind of faith community the kind where groupiness happens every evening in every room of every parish facility?

Hardly. Yet this is the ideal that is *au courant*. In certain circles, at least. We live in an era of radical loneliness. Many people crave close human interaction. We have our groups for just about everything, from therapy-oriented groups to groups of people who have nothing in common except ownership of a particular kind of automobile. We have people who share an enthusiasm for square dancing, and we have people who get together to try to figure out what it means to be male or female. Women having marathon "sharing" sessions. Men tramping out into a forest to don loin cloths, sit around a campfire, and pound on drums. The list is virtually endless.

The Catholic understanding of community is much broader and deeper than this. Catholicism finds joy in community in several ways, and all of them take for granted the truth of T. S. Eliot's words: "There is no life that is not in community, / And no community not lived in praise of God."

If you visit a Catholic parish church for Mass on a Sunday morning or Saturday evening and no one grabs your hand to pump it enthusiastically the second you walk through the door, don't be offended. If you find that you must simply walk into a quiet church and find yourself a pew to occupy, don't take it personally. If it happens to be a weekday, and the gathering is sparse, and you have plenty of empty space around you, remain calm. This is a good opportunity to experience the Catholic joy of community at a more than superficial level. The simple fact that folks are there, praying the liturgy *together* is not to be dismissed lightly. There can be a deep sense of companionship in this experience for those who unite themselves in prayer.

T. S. Eliot continues his poem thus: "Even the anchorite who meditates alone, / For whom the days and nights repeat the praise of God, / Prays for the Church, the Body of Christ incarnate."

In other words there is more to a Catholic faith community than what merely meets the eye. The basis for the joy of community is sharing in the one Holy Spirit. Even a hermit in an isolated hut participates in the joy of community, the community that is the Catholic people. The basis for the joy of community is not looking at each other so much as it is looking together toward a common goal. For Catholics, this common goal is the kingdom, or reign, of God. For Catholics, this common focus is the presence of the risen Christ in our midst.

Sometimes today people scoff at the pre–Vatican II liturgical set-up. During Mass, the priest did not face the people as he does today. Instead, priest and congregation all faced in the same direction, toward the altar. The common orientation of priest and congregation was toward the altar; that was the liturgical focal point. Scoffers say, well, in those days the priest had his back to the people, and the people all had their backs to one another. That's one way to look at it.

Another way to view the old arrangement is to see that the people attending Mass, while very much together, were involved in a community orientation away from and outside of themselves. The focus was out, not in. Scoffers of another stripe might charge that today's liturgical arrangement suggests an exercise in communal navel-gazing. Look at us, looking at one another. We love us, we love us.

The old way manifested one legitimate form of communal worship, everyone focused together on the eucharistic action on the altar. It gave us a genuine form of communal joy because we did what we did *together*. We gathered in church together, and we attended to the Mass together. There could be — not that there always was — an authentic feeling, if you will, of spiritual togetherness.

The new way manifests another form of communal worship, the ideal being communal attention to the presence of the risen Christ in our midst as the heart of the liturgical actions around the altar. This, too, can — not that it always does — give a genuine form of communal joy. Regardless, in both cases the operative understanding of community is more culturally than theologically driven. Or rather, cultural forces shape theological reflection.

In "the old days," one of the main supports for the dominant culture was "rugged individualism." The secular culture took for granted the power and legitimacy of self-reliance. Certainly people got together for various purposes, but the craving people feel today to share a communal intimacy involving "deep personal sharing" would have been alien to North Americans during, roughly, the first half of the twentieth century.

Because the cultural ethos of self-reliance was so popular, North American Catholics of the 1920s through the early 1960s were perfectly comfortable with everyone in church, the priest included, facing the same direction with the focus on the liturgical actions on the altar. But the cultural ethos underwent a major shift beginning in the 1960s. Rather suddenly — and for reasons too complex to discuss here — many people, including Catholics, began to feel a sense of social alienation. Therefore, people began to crave experiences of "togetherness" earlier decades knew nothing about.

In the same poem quoted above, T. S. Eliot had already critiqued the old ethos of self-reliance and individualism: "And now you live dispersed on ribbon roads, / And no man knows or cares who is his neighbour / Unless his neighbour makes too much disturbance, / But all dash to and fro in motor cars, / Familiar with the roads and settled nowhere."

A reaction developed to the old ethos of self-reliance and individualism, and that reaction gave birth to everything from sensitivity training to encounter groups to "support groups" of many kinds. Among Catholics, one liturgical reaction was to turn the altar around so the priest faces the congregation. In many newer Catholic parish churches, the congregation finds itself gathered in a semicircle facing not only the priest but itself as well. Liturgical coziness is the model. The God we worship is in our midst, not distant or far-removed. God is transcendent, yes, but transcendent to the point of radical intimacy with Creation and with His people. This is the ideal. Not that changing the interior arrangement of church furniture automatically accomplishes this ideal, of course, but at least it lends itself to the cultivation of the ideal.

In some Catholic churches, you will find the liturgy itself shaped by the cultural craving for human interaction, the need many people feel for a human touch, a hug, a kind word. In some parishes, for example, when it is time for the liturgical sharing of a sign of peace, the congregation erupts into a barely restrained chaos of hugging, hand-shaking, back-slapping, and visiting. This may continue for five or ten minutes, people milling about sharing a "sign of peace" with as many other people as possible.

Such liturgical experiences are symptomatic of our times, and there can be joy in such experiences. This is one thing many people need today from the Eucharist, so this is what they get, and it's a good example of culture shaping liturgy. This never would have happened in the 1940s or '50s, but it does happen today, a communal joy that is distinctly Catholic. But the parish is not the only — or even the most basic — locale for the joy of community to happen.

Everyone, Catholic or not, tends to assume that the parish is the most basic form of Catholic faith community. The communal bottom line you might say. We think in terms of a pyramid with the Vatican at the top and the parishes at the base. But for Catholicism the joy of community is rooted in a form of community life even more fundamental than the parish.

As much as we crave community today there is something we crave even more. We hunger from our heart and soul for the simple joys of family life. God knows we do.

Watch the next time you drive around the place where you live in the world. Keep a weather eye cocked. Look more closely than you ordinarily do at billboards, reader boards, and signs on or near buildings that announce the names of the businesses therein.

You will see, I promise, countless cases where advertisers use the word "family" or images from family life either to sell a product or service and/or to modify our perception of a product or service.

There seem to be no more general dentistry practices;, they all became "family dentistry." Automobile companies advertise vans and station wagons by plastering pictures on billboards and in magazines of impossibly perfect, impossibly happy families standing around their brand new vehicle. There are countless "family restaurants" nowadays. Financial institutions advertise their services using slogans such as "the friend of the family." They use warm, intimate terms such as "trust," "reliability," "neighbor," and "fidelity" — all terms we associate with family life.

You get the drift. We crave family life, or at least we crave what we imagine family life should be. Advertisers know this, they aren't stupid, they do their homework, and they use the language and images of family life to sell us stuff. Drink Brewski beer and you will have friends. Buy this station wagon and you will have a warm, conflict-free family. Our dentistry is painless because it's family dentistry. (Do we all climb into the chair together, or what?) You can trust our insurance company or bank because we are your friend, and if you use our services your family will be secure beyond belief. And so forth...

Contrary to the ways the secular culture uses family life, Catholicism insists that only family life can give us family life, and in family life is life's most basic experience of the joy of community. So seriously does Catholicism take this, that the church's understanding of itself includes the conviction that family life is the most basic form of faith community in the church. And in this community there is joy.

There is joy because this means that we need not look other places for life's deepest, most meaningful experiences. The potential for joy is greatest in our own homes and in our own back yards. Families exist because they offer the most important, most foundational experiences of spiritual joy. This is not a new idea; it's ancient. But it is one that Catholics recently rediscovered, and gradually it is taking hold and making a significant difference in the church's self-understanding. Slowly but surely. It, too, is a response to a cultural shift.

In his poem T. S. Eliot continues his critique of basic social networks: "Nor does the family even move about together, / But every son would have his motor cycle, / And daughters ride away on casual pillions" (*Dictionary service provided at no extra cost: In Eliot's poem a "pillion" is the pad or seat for an extra rider behind the saddle on a motorcycle*).

We live in a time when family life is stressed and fragmented beyond T. S. Eliot's wildest nightmares. Not only do adolescent sons and daughters tend to think of their homes as refueling stations and their parents as a necessary pain in the neck, but families struggle to keep themselves together from the moment a young couple marries. Jobs take up huge chunks of time, so wife and husband must make extra efforts simply to spend time together. Once children are born, frequently financial realities make it necessary for both parents to work, so children end up in day care situations that are often a far cry from Mom and Dad.

Soon children are in school all day while parents work all day. During summer vacations, children may be home alone, or they go into a day care facility. The family is not together; parents are not the primary influence on their children. Many of the social evils we are all aware of can be traced to the breakdown of family life, and frequently the breakdown of family life can be traced to economic and political injustices.

At the same time, television, movies, and the other secular media dilute parental and religious influences. Wild things can happen to children. Even kids from the best, healthiest families may experiment with dangerous addictive drugs, including alcohol, nicotine, and marijuana. Sad to say.

As far as Catholicism is concerned, the answer is to revive the joy of community that can happen most naturally in families. The social threats to family life are real, but relatively strong, healthy families can meet these threats, work through them, and emerge stronger on the other side. The joy of community appropriate to families is not a Good Ship Lollipop kind of joy. Rather, it's an underlying, consistent source of energy and resilience that enables the family to cope with stress, confront challenges, and face up to threats to the family's health and integrity without falling apart in the process. It is a joy that comes from knowing in one's bones that here, in my family, I am loved, accepted, forgiven, and always welcome.

It is the task of parish communities to draw on all their resources to support and reinvigorate family life so families will have the deep joy that is their strength to draw upon. "Each parish must be fully committed" to the pastoral care of families, said Pope John Paul II during a visit to the United States, "especially in the face of so much breakdown and undermining of family life in society."

But there is still more to say about the joy of community. There is a form of community that sometimes develops between the family and the parish. It's a communal way station between the two, if you will. Many Catholics discover that in today's church and today's society they find much joy through participation in a small faith community of one kind or another. In some instances, parish leaders organize the parish into smaller communities that gather regularly for spiritual, social, educational, and service-oriented purposes. In other cases, groups of Catholics simply organize their own small community. In either situation the main purpose is to provide people with the opportunity to get to know a group of people with whom they can share their faith. Often the parish community is too large to allow for getting to know other people, but in a smaller community this is possible.

The joy people find in a small faith community comes from sharing the joy and anguish in their daily lives. Great joy can come from simply gathering with ten or twelve other people, now and then, for informal group prayer. Great joy can come from gathering with a few others once or twice a month to listen to and talk with one another about the "gut issues" in our lives. St. Paul calls it sharing one another's burdens. We need to do this, and when we do it nourishes in us the energy and strength that comes from deep spiritual joy.

So important is this that St. Paul equated it with fulfillment of the law of love articulated by Jesus: "Bear one another's burdens, and in this way you will fulfill the law of Christ" (Gal. 6:2).

Underlying the Catholic joy of community, regardless of the form it takes, is a basic dictum of Jesus, a teaching so familiar to us that we may no longer comprehend what it means. Listen closely, closely. Matthew's Jesus puts it like this: "'You shall love the Lord your God with all your heart, and with all your soul, and with all your mind.' This is the greatest and first commandment. And a second is like [the Greek word means, literally, "the same as"] it: 'You shall love your neighbor as yourself'" (22:37–39).

Do not skim lightly over these words of Jesus. You have read them so many, many times. You have heard them so many, many times. Times beyond number. But now read them again carefully, slowly, and let them sink into your heart. Only then can you hear these words in spirit and truth. Read with your heart, not just with your eyes.

In this saying of Jesus we discover the ultimate foundation for the joy of community. Here is the holy secret: The closest we will ever get to God in this world is the people we live and work with. To be with them is to be with God. To love them not just in word but in action is to love God. Yes! Difficult to believe, I know. A tough nut to crack. But true! Those ne'er-do-wells in our family, those irritating goofs at work. In them we find God; therefore, this is where we find the deep joy of community.

Don't despair. I know. Family life can make you go bananas. The people you work with are enough, sometimes, to make you want to go into the nearest closet, close the door, and scream. Sometimes you feel so bad you could eat worms. But don't give up. This is the spiritual heartland. Our relationships with the irritating people we live and work with are where we find or do not find God. If we find God here we are set for life and for all eternity. If we find God at home and at work we find God everyplace.

But there is no "if." You don't have to find God at home because God is already there longing for you with passionate love. The Creator of the universe is already there, at home and at work, trying to get your attention. Knock, knock, anybody home? The risen Christ is already there, ready to work through your honest efforts to cope with the anguish and celebrate the joys (cross and resurrection) of family life. The risen Christ is already there in your workplace, ready to work through your honest efforts to do your best at whatever you do. In all of this you will find the deep joy of community.

Karl Rahner, who wrote books that are difficult to understand, was probably the greatest Catholic theologian of the twentieth century. He explained the saying of Jesus quoted back a few paragraphs ago. It means, he said, that we cannot separate our relationship with God from our relationships with other people, especially the people we encounter most often and most directly. Love your neighbor, love God. Love God, love your neighbor. This is why the joy of community is possible and happens, because in our human relationships we experience the Divine Mystery. And because in our loving intimacy with God we also encounter those we live and work with.

This is the heartland, the spiritual heartland of the Christian life. Think about it and rejoice. Know that God's deep, abiding, absolutely reliable love is with you in your most significant human relationships and your most casual human interactions. In your roles as spouse, parent, worker, and friend. In the briefest encounter with a supermarket clerk or convenience store attendant. Know that God's deep, abiding, absolutely reliable love is with you on the brink of despair, riding a wave of happiness, or anyplace in between. Never doubt that, for nothing is more certain in this world or the next.

The joy of community is the joy that comes from finding and feeling God's love in our relationships with other people, pilgrims all, like ourselves. God knows.

The Catholic joy of community is both "micro" and "macro," little and big, local and universal. We find the joy of community in a small faith community, a local parish community, and a regional faith community called a diocese. But for Catholics the joy of community ultimately includes the entire Roman Catholic community worldwide and, in a secondary but very real way, the entire Christian community all over the world. It even includes, in a genuine sense, non-Christians and even non-believers. In words from the Second Vatican Council's *Declaration on the Relation of the Church to Non-Christian Religions:*

> All [people] form but one community. This is so because all stem from the one stock which God created to people the entire earth, and also because all share a common destiny, namely God. His providence, evident goodness, and saving designs extend to all [people] against the day when the elect are gathered together in the holy city which is illumined by the glory of God, and in whose splendor all peoples will walk. (no. 1)

Catholics think of themselves as part of a worldwide human community. In particular, however, we belong in a special way to our worldwide Catholic community. When a pope dies, for example, and a new Pope is elected, Catholics all over the world take a personal interest. Among other things, the pope is a symbol of our worldwide unity as a community of faith. There is a special sense of joy in visiting Rome, St. Peter's Basilica, and the Vatican, because these too are symbols of our unity as a people scattered the world over.

Because we belong to a worldwide community of faith, the joy of Catholic community is more than personal and local. We can't think of ourselves merely in personal or local terms. When an adult becomes a Catholic, he or she pledges membership in the universal Catholic Church, not just membership in a local parish community. That's the "macro" dimension of the Catholic joy of community.

The joy of belonging to a worldwide Catholic community has an impact on many dimensions of Catholic life. You will find many unique characteristics among Catholic parishes but also many similarities. All Catholic parishes use the same Lectionary, for example, the collection of scriptural readings used during the Eucharist. All Catholic parishes use the same Roman Missal, the collection of prayers used for the Eucharist itself. Any parish that — out of a certain spiritual arrogance, one might say — chooses to use different, perhaps locally written, prayers for the Mass, incidental though it may seem, distances itself in a way from the worldwide Catholic community. Incidental though it may seem, such a parish diminishes its sense of joy at belonging to the universal church. Yes, even the details matter.

It all boils down to the Catholic conviction that we are not meant to be in the world alone. We are not meant to go our way as isolated individuals. Rather, our Creator wants us to be with one another. This is not, however, a blueprint for a mutual admiration society. Hardly.

Any Christian community requires us not only to love those who love us. No. It gets more difficult than that. We are to love even those who do not love us. Our "enemies" we must love, as well. A hard saying, it's true. Ponder the following words of Luke's Jesus. They are among the most important, most appealing, and most challenging words in the entire New Testament. Read these words of Jesus at least twice before moving on, at least twice:

> But I say to you that listen, Love your enemies, do good to those who hate you, bless those who curse you, pray for those who abuse you.
>
> If anyone strikes you on the cheek, offer the other also; and from anyone who takes away your coat do not withhold even your shirt. Give to everyone who begs from you; and if anyone takes away your goods, do not ask for them again. Do to others as you would have them do to you.
>
> If you love those who love you, what credit is that to you? For even sinners love those who love them. If you do good to those who do good to you, what credit is that to you? For even sinners do the same. If you lend to those from whom

you hope to receive, what credit is that to you? Even sinners
lend to sinners, to receive as much again. But love your enemies, do good, and lend, expecting nothing in return. Your
reward will be great, and you will be children of the Most
High; for he is kind to the ungrateful and the wicked. Be
merciful, just as your Father is merciful.

Do not judge, and you will not be judged; do not con-
demn, and you will not be condemned. Forgive, and you
will be forgiven; give, and it will be given to you. A good
measure, pressed down, shaken together, running over, will
be put into your lap; for the measure you give will be the
measure you get back. (6:27–38)

How a Catholic community responds to these sayings of Jesus
says a great deal about the quality of faith in that community,
the quality of that community's intimacy with the risen Lord,
the quality of the joy you will find there. These words of Jesus
apply to every form of Catholic community, and they inspire
meditation and prayer.

What does it mean to love a two-year-old who is driving you
to distraction? What does it mean to love a teenager who is
clearly the enemy of the day? What does it mean to love a pas-
tor or lay administrator whose decisions stifle community spirit?
What does it mean to love a spouse or co-worker who is a major
source of irritation? No easy answers, but in the struggle to find
answers we find the joy of community.

There is a deeper joy, in a faith community, in loving those
who are difficult to love. In a very real sense, we only begin
to experience the depths of Christian community when we embrace these most difficult words of Jesus and make them the basis
for our life together. A Catholic community with an active love
for those who are hard to love is a Catholic community indeed.
Whether we talk about a family, a small faith community, a parish community, a diocesan community, or the community of the
workplace, the Lord of the universe calls us to will the good of
those who are most difficult to love.

If we do not will and work for the good of those who are difficult to love, our community is something less than fully Catholic,
and our joy is something less than it can be. But in a community
of faith that wills and works for the good of those who are "the
enemy," the joy of community will be deeper and stronger than
anyplace else in the world.

CHAPTER FOUR

The Joy of the Saints

There is a wonderful novel called *Time and Again,* by Jack Finney (Simon and Schuster, 1970). In this story a hush-hush agency with connections to the U.S. government recruits the novel's main character, Simon Morley, to participate in a marvelous experiment. Si agrees, and before long he finds himself a traveler in time. There are no "time machines" in this story; the process of returning to the past is accomplished in a quiet, almost poetic fashion. After days and days of waiting, Simon simply looks out his apartment window one night to discover that he has slipped back nearly a hundred years. He visits the New York City of 1882 and meets people who, in his own time, had died long ago — living, breathing human beings with real lives. He is fascinated by their faces, by their humanity.

Si Morley's journey back to the late 1800s is based on Alfred Einstein's theory of time. Einstein suggested that we in the present are like people drifting along a winding river. We can see the present, but the past and the future are hidden from view around the curves in the river of time. Still, the past and future are real. Those who arrange Si's trip back to 1882 ask themselves if it might be possible to get out of the boat and walk back around the bend to the past. And, for the fictional character Simon Morley, it works.

Catholicism has a similar belief, but it is not fictional. It is real, and it is about the connection between time and eternity, not past, present, and future. Catholics have this "crazy idea" that when people die they do not cease to exist. It's a marvelous idea that faith experience tells us is true. Not only is it a doctrine of our faith, but empirical data gathered in recent years reveals that a great many people experience the "presence" of deceased loved ones.

There is continuity between this life and another, better life called "eternal." Of course, "eternal" and "eternity" are words we use to talk about a reality that escapes the grasp of the human intellect. "Eternal" life is not a concept of time at all. It is a word we use to talk about the life that awaits us after the life we flounder around in here and now.

The point is simply that personal relationships — the community we discussed in the last chapter — transcend or go beyond time and space. Catholicism is not just a religious tradition. The Catholic Church is not just an institution, albeit the oldest institution in the Western world. The church is primarily a faith community, a community that exists both here and there, now and then. We continue in relationship with those who have "passed on" to "the other side." What a joy! The Catholic term for this reality is "the communion of saints." We remain "in communion" with loved ones no longer navigating the river of time.

In the words of theologian Richard McBrien, the church is not just any community.

> It is a community of those who have been transformed by Christ and the Holy Spirit and who have explicitly and thankfully acknowledged the source of that transformation. Since transformation is a process, to be completed when the Kingdom of God is fully realized at the end of history, our bond in Christ and the Spirit is not broken by death. (*Catholicism*, new edition [HarperSanFrancisco, 1994], 1105–6)

Of course, I use "mystery" in the religious and theological sense. We're not talking about Agatha Christie "whodunits." Theologically, "mystery" means something that opens up and reveals an invisible divine reality. A religious "mystery," is something we can see, taste, touch, hear, and/or smell that brings us into the invisible presence of God.

"Mystery" is close to what we mean by "sacrament." All kinds of things can be religious mysteries, including words, places, people, concepts, and objects. "Communion of saints" is a mystery in this sense; it's a concept that brings us into the hidden presence of a divine reality, namely, our ongoing relationship with those who have gone before us into "eternity."

This knocks our standard, taken-for-granted scientific frame of mind for a couple of loops. If we are honest, we must admit that we are skeptical about the existence of anything we can't see. Period. Yet here comes Catholicism asking us to believe in the existence of an invisible community to which we belong. We are likely to be skeptical in the extreme.

As long as we cling to our scientific presuppositions as the only path to legitimate human knowledge, we will have trouble. But look what's going on here. Science asks us to take it on a kind of faith that nothing can exist unless we can verify its existence by scientific methods. No scientist can prove to you that this presupposition is true. Either you accept it or you don't, and because most people accept it we accept it too.

Catholicism says, yes, scientific methods result in valid forms of knowing. And there can be joy in this knowing. But science has its limits. There are other legitimate forms of knowledge. In particular, there is the kind of knowledge based on human experience of divine but invisible realities. People experience these realities and find joy in them. This kind of human experience is valid too. Can't prove it to you, just as science can't prove its presupposition. Either you consult your own experience and the community's experience and accept this. Or you don't.

Catholicism says that sometimes seeing is believing. Quite so. But sometimes it's just the reverse. Sometimes believing is seeing. Sometimes faith — human intuitions of the invisible presence of divine realities — leads us to "see," not with our physical eyes but with heart and soul. Heart and soul can see too, you know. Heart and soul can see if we throw wide the doors of human perception and allow them to see. Heart and soul can see with the eyes of faith, a faith based on human experience of hidden realities. And there is joy in this experience.

It is with the eyes of our spirit that we can see the communion of saints, the community that exists beyond time and space. Catholics find joy in their knowledge and experience of ongoing friendship or loving intimacy with those who no longer thrash around in the river of time and the bubble of space. There is joy in continuing our loving intimacy with loved ones who have gone ahead of us. These people are "saints" in the way that St. Paul used the term to refer to all believers, here and there. "I have heard of your faith in the Lord Jesus," Paul writes to the Ephesians, "and your love toward all the saints" (1:15).

There is joy in cultivating friendships with people whose goodness and common sense are acknowledged officially by the community of faith in this world. We call these people "saints" when they are "canonized" by the church, but they are imperfect people who did ordinary things extraordinarily well. Also, since passing into eternity they have shown themselves to be more than ordinarily interested in and involved with the community of faith still on pilgrimage in this world. Just as we help one another by our prayers in this world, so those in eternity may continue to help us by their prayers and we may continue to pray to them, asking for their assistance in matters large and small.

So we have friends "in eternity" who are friends indeed. There is joy in this realization, the joy of the saints. The "communion of saints" means that the community we belong to is not limited by time and space. It exists in this world, but it knows no bounds.

At this point, we must ask one of the most important theological questions anyone can ask: So what? So people continue to exist on the other side of dusty death. So what? So we belong to a community that transcends here and now. So what? So this: Because we believe in and experience the communion of saints, we are never alone. Sometimes philosophers wag a finger in the air and declare that, yes, everyone dies alone. But no, Catholicism insists — a twinkle of joy in its eye — even in death we are never alone. In a flash, a mere fraction of a second, the dying person is in the company of loved ones he or she knew in this world. Imagine that. Go ahead, imagine that.

The Catholic belief in the communion of saints is not only a comfort, however. It is not only reassuring. It is also a challenge. Consider this. If we find joy in being members of a community that goes on into eternity, that puts what happens in this life in a different light. Does it not? All of a sudden, all our thrashing around "here below" takes on less than ultimate value. Our sorrows have less power to darken our lives. Our joys become but a hint of a joy to come. Human suffering is not the end, and human rejoicing is small potatoes.

"Eternal life" is not just a future reality, something we look forward to after we cross the Great Divide. Catholicism is not about "pie in the sky when we die by and by." Rather, Catholicism takes great joy in its experience that eternal life begins now. Here and now. The joys of this life increase because they are, even now, a share in eternal joy. The pain and anguish of this life take on hidden meanings because their power over us is not final.

This is a perspective with tremendous appeal to the people of our time. Best-selling books are written by people who were clinically "dead" and claim they experienced the afterlife and returned to tell the story. Whether true or fanciful fiction, these books sell because people long for reassurance that they need not fear death or what happens after death. The risk, of course, is that readers of such books may become preoccupied with "the afterlife" to the neglect of this life.

The Catholic belief in the communion of saints short-circuits such a preoccupation because it affirms the value of this life. We receive this life as a gift, and through Baptism we share even now in that better life called "eternal." People become officially canonized saints, take note, not because they spurned this life and this world, but because they embraced them. People are considered "holy" who embrace the life God gives them and use it to actively love God and neighbor in the knockabout world.

St. Francis of Assisi is perhaps the most popular officially canonized saint of all time. We call him holy because he loved and
embraced the life God gave him, and because he loved and celebrated all of God's Creation. Saints love their neighbors; they
don't try to avoid them. Saints embrace life; they don't reject it.
Saints don't seek out suffering, but if they must suffer they accept
it with something like equanimity, giving witness to their experience that in this life even suffering has a life-giving purpose and
mysteriously serves the cause of life.

The joyful challenge of the communion of saints, then, is to
live life to the last drop. The joyful challenge of the communion
of saints is to say "Yes!" to whatever life we find ourselves with,
"Yes!" to the gift from God that I am for myself and for others.
To say yes to myself and my life is to say yes to God, and to say
yes to God is to know joy.

But there is more to the challenge of the communion of saints.
If we all belong to the communion of saints, there is no room for
injustice or violence. The communion of saints calls us to actively
oppose violence and injustice because in the communion of saints
we are all brothers and sisters. The communion of saints is not
only a reality existing beyond this world, it is also a goal we strive
for in this world, to include all people as equal members. Therefore, Catholics can't help but apply their faith to political and
economic issues. There is this joy. Our faith is alien to nothing; it
has to do with everything. This, too, is the joy of the communion
of saints.

For now, the communion of saints is a present reality and a
contemporary concern, and it leads us to some kind of humility.
We find ourselves smack in the middle of a community in this
world that is far from perfect, yet we embrace it because it is the
communion of saints. Here in this imperfect community of faith
we find the gift of spiritual liberation and healing. Call it salvation. Here, in this imperfect community of faith, we find even
now the beginnings of eternal life. So we try to put up with one
another, irritating and hard to live with as we are. It's all the joy
of the communion of saints. To paraphrase Father Andrew Gree-

ley, if you can find a perfect faith community, go ahead and join it. As soon as you do, however, it will be perfect no longer.

Sometimes, we must admit, it is precisely the communion of saints that non-Catholics find objectionable. Sad to say. Perhaps they visit a Catholic parish community, and what they find is a gathering of ordinary people. Nothing special at all. Where, they may ask themselves, are the glories of Catholicism? Maybe they visited the Vatican or saw it on television. Maybe they became intrigued by what they read in a book about the church. Who knows? For whatever reason, they decide to check out a local Catholic parish of a Sunday morning. And maybe what they find is a motley crew, heavy on the motley.

This is the communion of saints, at least the earthly contingent of it? Oh, my. People flailing about. Organizing this, organizing that. Maybe the liturgy is a disappointment. What's this about a second collection today for social concerns or the leak in the roof? What's this about elections for the parish council for which no one is running? What's this about a conflict on the liturgy committee? You call that a sermon — pardon me, homily? The Gospel reading was the Beatitudes from Jesus' Sermon on the Mount ("Blessed are the poor in spirit..."), and the homily was about needing more money to recarpet the church? There are factions in the parish, some wildly enthusiastic about their belief that the Blessed Virgin is appearing in an eastern European country; others wanting nothing to do with such stuff. I beg your pardon?

It's true. No getting around it. The communion of saints in this world is a motley crew. The typical Catholic parish community is at sixes and sevens about three-quarters of the time. It's enough to make you go bananas. Spiritually speaking, that is.

Ah, but the other one-quarter of the time life in that parish community is the sheerest, plainest heaven. There is no describing it, no describing it at all. Also, it's unpredictable. You never know, all you can do is hang around and wait for the joy. Before long, it will happen. The joy. Everything falls into place, and you know you're in the middle of the communion of saints. It may be noisy at the time, or it may be quiet. But you'll know. You'll know, and from then on you are more than willing to tolerate motley in order to wait for the next such experience or to help it to happen yourself.

It's a grace, that's all, a grace pure and simple.

The communion of saints includes all of us motley believers here and now, of course. But as noted above, it also includes the ones who have left motley behind. You know, the ones who now wear "dem golden slippers" to "walk dem golden streets." Catholicism finds much joy in its experience of the continuing presence of the saints, both loved ones we knew personally and those who have taken on a much wider significance for the church motley, the church on earth.

In particular, we take inspiration, encouragement, and guidance from the lives of canonized saints, stories about what they did and said during their own time of "motley-hood" on the earth. Some of these stories are factual and historically verifiable to the point of satisfying even the most scrupulous scientific mind. Others grow and bloom in the good soil of legend. In both cases, they are likely to offer us the most delightful truths.

Consider the aforementioned St. Francis of Assisi. Stories about St. Francis blend legend and fact in the most delicious way, and they are guaranteed to make you a better person if you read them. Unless you are an absolute, unreformed grump, if you read these stories you will be easier to live with, and you will smile more often. Many come from a collection known as *The Little Flowers of St. Francis*, including the story of St. Francis preaching to the birds and the story of St. Francis and the wolf of Gubbio.

We find the key to the *Little Flowers* in the very first sentence of the very first page. "First, it must be borne in mind that our blessed master Saint Francis in everything he did was like Christ." Every story, legendary, factual, or a mix of the two, is meant to show how St. Francis lived out the spirit of Jesus in his own time and culture. So if we read that St. Francis preached to the birds or converted a wolf to a life of gentleness and peace, this is more than a charming legend. There are lessons here for us as well. We have only to look for these lessons, and they will reveal themselves to us.

Take the wolf of Gubbio story. The *Little Flowers* tells us that "a fearful wolf, enormous in size and most ferocious in the savagery of his hunger," prowled about the region of Gubbio. "It had devoured not only animals but men and women too, so much that it held all the people in such terror that they all went armed whenever they went into the countryside as if they were off to grim war.... Such terror gripped them all that scarcely anyone dared to go outside the city gate."

St. Francis happens to be visiting Gubbio. He hears about the terrible wolf and decides to go out, meet the wolf, and see what he can do. The people of Gubbio caution Francis not to go outside the city, but he has no fear. Immediately, the fearsome wolf rushes toward the saint, showing his sharp teeth. Calling the wolf, St. Francis says, "Come to me, brother wolf, and in Christ's name I command you not to harm me or anybody."

Upon hearing this command, "like a lamb and not a wolf, with lowered head [the wolf] laid himself at the feet of the saint."

Only a pious legend? It is more than that. Much more. The *Little Flowers* was written hundreds of years ago, but the author was no fool. Even if the story is historical, think in terms of metaphors, or you'll miss the point entirely. What is the wolf in the story but anything that strikes fear in the human heart? What is the response of St. Francis but a reminder of the teaching of Christ?

Over and over in the Gospels, Jesus admonishes his disciples to stop being afraid. "Why are you afraid, you of little faith?" (Matt. 8:26). The story of the wolf of Gubbio is a reminder that when we are afraid of something, anything, if we face it with trust in God it will do us no ultimate harm. Though we stare death in the face — which we all do eventually — we need have no fear. We must leave the security of the city behind and go out to meet the wolf, but if we approach the beast with the risen Christ in our heart it will become tame.

There are countless stories from the lives of the saints; this is one of the joys of the communion of saints. In many instances, however, the saints themselves left behind writings that we may read. St. Francis of Assisi wrote his famous "Canticle to Brother Sun." St. John of the Cross and St. Teresa of Avila, in the sixteenth century, left behind tremendous works of mystical theology. St. Thomas Aquinas's thirteenth-century *Summa theologiae* continues to have a profound impact on theologians today. St. Catherine of Siena's fourteenth-century life was full of adventures, including getting pushy with popes, but she also wrote a book on mystical theology. As to the relevance of mysticism, hear G. K. Chesterton, a convert to Catholicism and one of the most quotable writers of the twentieth century: "The whole secret of mysticism is this: that man can understand everything by the help of what he does not understand."

St. Thérèse of Lisieux, a late nineteenth-century French Carmelite nun, left behind remarkable documents, including her autobiographical *Story of a Soul.* This pampered — one might call her "spoiled" — young woman from an affluent family lived her brief adult life in an obscure convent, yet through her writings she became one of the great spiritual guides of the century following her death. Thérèse said that she hated praying the Rosary, and she believed it was a sign of faith and trust in God to fall asleep during formal prayer times and not feel guilty about it later.

One of the great joys of being Catholic is knowing that we have countless companions on our way — in this world and the next — through our membership in the communion of saints. When we say that we belong to the communion of saints, all we mean is that we belong to a community much, much larger than the one we can see.

In his novel *Black Cherry Blues* (Little, Brown, 1989), crime fiction writer James Lee Burke, a Catholic, has his character Dave Robicheaux put it this way: "One of the advantages of being Catholic is that you belong to the western world's largest private club. Not all of its members are the best or most likable people, but many of them are."

Imagine that.

CHAPTER FIVE

The Joy of Sex

E. B. White, author of the modern children's classic *Charlotte's Web*, and humorist James Thurber once collaborated on a book. They dreamed up a great title: *Is Sex Necessary?* The Catholic response to this question is an unqualified, enthusiastic "Yes!" Not only is sex necessary, it is one of the Creator's most delightful ideas.

Can we talk about "Catholic sex"? Isn't sex the same for everyone? Good question. Actually, if recent empirical research is correct, married Catholics do have a unique experience of sex. In *Sex: The Catholic Experience* (Thomas More, 1994), Father Andrew Greeley summarizes the results of his sociological research: "Catholics have sex more often than do other Americans, they are more playful in their sexual relationships, and they seem to enjoy their sexual experiences more."

You have, no doubt, seen those bumper stickers: TEACHERS DO IT WITH CLASS. PRINTERS DO IT WITHOUT WRINKLING THE SHEETS. PILOTS DO IT IN MID-AIR. That sort of thing. Well, how about a new one: CATHOLICS DO IT WITH MORE JOY. As they say, "If you got it, flaunt it."

The Catholic joy of sex goes way back. You will find it reflected in the most ancient scriptural traditions. The Old Testament is never shy or ashamed about sex. One whole book, the Song of Songs, is erotic from beginning to end, although most English translations tone down certain explicit passages, which reveals a regrettable sense of shame in the translators that the original writer(s) knew nothing about. Scripture scholar Marvin H. Pope, in his *Anchor Bible* translation of the Song of Songs, has no such hesitations, giving these lines an accurate rendering. Thus:

A bundle of myrrh is my love to me,
Between my breasts he lodges.... (1:13)

My love thrust his "hand" [Hebrew euphemism for penis]
Into the hole,
And my inwards seethed for him.... (5:4)

How beautiful your sandaled feet,
O prince's daughter!
Your curvy thighs like ornaments
Crafted by artist hands.
Your vulva a rounded crater:
May it never lack punch!.... (7:2–3)

Let your breasts be like grape clusters,
The scent of your vulva like apples.... (7:9)

Now, good reader, whether you are Catholic or not, this line of discussion may surprise you. "I thought Catholicism had a kind of 'sex is dirty and dangerous' attitude," you may think. Well, you're right. And wrong. The honest truth is that some influential early theologians, most notably St. Augustine of Hippo (354–430) had negative attitudes toward sex. It is doubtful how much impact their views had on ordinary folks, however. Also, some of today's church leaders have mixed feelings about sex. Father Greeley says that Catholics have better sex "despite the repressive stance of the leadership of the Church on marital sex."

The truth is that the overwhelming majority of married Catholics are in a different space, when it comes to sex, than are the church's leaders. So it goes. Maybe someday the church's leaders will get together with the church on this. The most important thing to be aware of is that married Catholics, in general, find a great deal of joy in sex, even if some of the highest members of the hierarchy would blush to hear it. In this case, the people are more in tune with the living Catholic tradition than are some members of the hierarchy.

At the same time please take note that even in modern official church documents married people are encouraged to contribute to the church's understanding of marriage and sex. Pope John Paul II, in *Familiaris Consortio,* a 1981 "apostolic exhortation" on family life, wrote:

> Christian spouses and parents can and should offer their unique and irreplaceable contribution to the elaboration of an authentic evangelical discernment in the various situations and cultures in which men and women live their marriage and their family life. They are qualified for the role by their charisma or specific gift, the gift of the sacrament of matrimony.

This is what we are about, so many married Catholics today. Drawing upon our "charism or specific gift," we offer our "unique and irreplaceable contribution" to the church's reflections on the meaning of sex and marriage and the joys thereof. Sooner or later, I do believe the message will get through from married Catholics to the church's leaders. In the meantime, the joy of Catholic sex continues.

Sex and babies, that's what you may think of as the Catholic perspective on sex. You may think that for Catholicism, sex is for making babies, and that's about it. Certainly there is joy in bringing new little people into the world, and most Catholic couples do this. But egad, most sex in marriage is for the sheer joy of it.

The most common purpose of sex is not to have babies; the most frequent purpose of sex is to nourish married love. Indeed, most Catholic couples would say that unless they enjoy sex frequently and allow its joyful pleasures to nourish the bond between husband and wife, they are not being responsible parents. Children, after all, need parents whose love is living and resilient. They need parents who are in love with each other, passionately in love with each other. For Catholics, now and then the theme is sex and babies. Mostly, however, the theme is sex and love, sweet, sweet sex and love.

The Catholic joy of sex comes not just from — to put it quaintly — the pleasures of the marriage bed. The Catholic joy of sex comes from our experience that when spouses make love something bigger than the two of them happens. Indeed, this most physical way to express our love for each other is also the most spiritual way. This comes from the Catholic conviction that we are not just bodies with souls rattling around inside us someplace. Like a BB in a boxcar, you might say. The body is not just a temporary home for the soul. Rather, as we have noted before, in the words of theologian Karl Rahner, we are "embodied spirits."

Anything that affects the body affects the soul. Anything that affects the soul affects the body. So sex is not just a physical activity; it is a profoundly spiritual activity at the same time. Sex in marriage is a spiritual exercise. Sex brings husband and wife closer to each other emotionally and spiritually. But it also brings husband and wife closer to God.

Loving sex with no intention to conceive a baby is a deeply spiritual, deeply joyful activity. Sex feels good, and it's fun, and that's the way the Creator means it to be. Do it till you drop, that's the Catholic perspective on sex, and there is nothing hedonistic about this. Here is the point: It's just as important to the couple's marital spirituality to make love regularly as it is important to a basic Catholic spirituality to receive Holy Communion regularly. In this sense, in a healthy Catholic marriage sex is a kind of sacrament that nourishes both human and divine love in the marriage.

But is this not an irresponsible point of view? If we announce such a perspective, won't teenagers go wild for one another's bodies? On the contrary. If anything, being open and honest about the joys of married sex will help the world at large to see that it is precisely *marriage* that makes sex joyful. It is only in a loving marriage that sex "works" the way it is supposed to work. It is only in a loving marriage that sex becomes the deeply pleasurable, spiritually satisfying experience God designed it to be.

Catholicism and sex go together well, contrary to the popular myth that Catholics are guilt-ridden about sex. Not that this hasn't happened, of course, but if we're talking about a healthy understanding of Catholicism, then it can only fit with healthy attitudes about sex. As Father Greeley points out, the "stories" basic to Catholicism carry warm religious images, and the "stories" implicit in the warm religious images "are stories of fidelity, commitment, of promises made, honored, and kept permanently." Therefore, Father Greeley suggests, the more people hear and meditate upon the warm religious images of their Catholic tradition, the less likely they are to become sexually active before marriage and the more likely they are to remain faithful in marriage for a lifetime.

Apart from this, however, Catholicism insists on the connection between joy, sex, and marriage for some very practical reasons. Let's take a bit of a side trip, here, but an important one.

Today, what used to be called "shacking up" is socially acceptable. In fact, conventional wisdom insists that "living together" is the best way to get to know each other before marriage, make a better marital choice, and lay a solid foundation for marriage.

Catholicism insists that anyone who buys this line of thought makes a mistake. A huge mistake, in fact. Because cohabitation and premarital sex are so taken for granted today, and they constitute a major threat to the future of joyful Catholic sex, it is well to include some discussion of this topic.

The Christian tradition that views premarital sex and premarital cohabitation as sinful is rooted in some common sense that seems scarce these days. If cohabitation and/or premarital sex are sinful, it's because they are bad for people and bad for relationships. If there are traditional prohibitions against such choices, it's because they constitute a good way to mess up a perfectly good relationship. It puts the joy of marriage and the joy of married sex at risk. Plain and simple. In her outstanding book *Ten Stupid Things Women Do to Mess Up Their Lives* (Villard Books, 1994), psychologist Dr. Laura Schlessinger offers a fine summary of reasons that support this traditional Christian perspective:

- **Couples who cohabit with their future spouses have a higher divorce rate than those who do not.** Psychologist David G. Myers, Ph.D., author of *The Pursuit of Happiness* (William Morrow & Co., 1992), discusses three national studies. One survey of 13,000 adults found that couples who lived together before marriage were one-third more likely to separate or divorce within ten years. A Canadian survey of 5,300 women revealed that the ones who cohabited were 54 percent more likely to divorce within fifteen years. Finally, a Swedish study of 4,300 women found living together before marriage linked to an 80 percent greater risk of divorce.

    The tradition of an engagement period developed for a good reason, namely, that couples need a time before they marry and live together to deepen their relationship in nongenital ways. Sex can easily short-circuit this necessary development before marriage.

- **Cohabiting is playing Russian roulette with your life.** It's true that not every couple who cohabits before marriage will end up divorced. But the odds are not in a given couple's favor. So why take chances? Why be eager to play Russian roulette with your life? Fear of not having a life if someone won't marry you is not a good reason. There is much wisdom in a choice to wait and grow in maturity, independence, and security-of-self.

- **Cohabitation can retard personal progress toward maturity.** Every young person's primary task is to grow in self-esteem and a sense of competence, so that when he or she chooses someone to marry it won't be out of a desperate need to heal the hurts that come from the past. Marriage should come as a choice to share oneself and one's life experience. Cohabitation does not contribute to personal maturity, especially for people from a troubled family background.

- **No one can bypass the hard work of growing up.** Sometimes cohabiting couples fantasize that by "living together" they can find out who they are and what they want to do with their lives. Wrong way around. Only people who first do the hard work of establishing who they are, what they believe in, and what they want from life are likely to marry successfully.

- **Denial is a big part of "living together."** Denial invariably plays a big part in the choice to cohabit, from denial of one's own true needs to denial of what the other person is about. "I can be different," or "I can change him/her" are common statements from cohabiting persons.

- **Cohabitation is not the way to make someone love you.** To move in with someone when you are not sure how he or she feels about you is an attempt to manipulate him or her. "If we live together maybe he/she will begin to really love me." To do this is to agree to audition for someone. What often happens is that both people end up feeling bad about themselves.

- **"Living together" proves nothing.** All living together may prove is that you can live together. Cohabitation is not marriage, all it can prove is that you can cohabit. It does not prove you can be married. Ask any couple who cohabited before marriage; they will tell you that marriage does, indeed, make a big difference.

- **Living-in may equal giving-in.** Young people often miss the point that a strong sense of self and satisfaction with one's life is centered in the will to overcome circumstances, not to give in to being overcome by anyone or anything. People who cohabit often think they have no other alternatives. Instead, they should use their courage and creativity in ways that make them choosers, not beggars.

- **Cohabitation often means settling for less.** A young woman or man who wants respect from their "significant other" should never settle for or permit less. If the other insists on "living together" and/or being sexually active before marriage, that's a huge red flag for the future of your relationship.

- **"Living together" sends a clear message to your partner.** When you move in with no public commitment, no ring, no wedding license and no wedding, the other knows that he or she needs to do very little to get you. This means that you don't place a high value on what you're giving — your very self.

- **Cohabitation is a sign of personal immaturity.** This is the reason couples who "live together" are more likely to divorce. They tend to be impatient and unable to postpone gratification. When a person is unwilling to put in the time and effort to built a solid foundation, he or she is usually not the type who, later, will be able persist with the effort and sacrifice needed to develop a marriage and keep it growing for fifty or sixty years. Insisting on sex before marriage and "living together" are the choices of basically immature people, those who say, in effect, "I want it, and I want it now, and I'm going to hold my breath until I turn blue if I can't have it NOW!" Sometimes this is coupled with fear of commitment for whatever reasons. "Let's play it safe, just in case." The trouble is, "playing it safe" can bring disastrous results.

Dr. Schlessinger summarizes thus:

People have problems. There are no relationships without problems. The issue is whether people have the maturity and the commitment to hang in there with each other and work out the problems. Or do they have the inner strength and courage to admit a mistake and let go. That's what makes the difference.

A living-in arrangement does not inherently have that kind of commitment; nor is it a further step in that direction. Living-in is more a convenience and a fantasy; typically the former for men, the latter for women. As you've surely guessed by now, I'm very agin' it. Let's get pragmatic: Statistics show that living-in doesn't ensure a quality, long-lasting marriage, probably because the attitude of one of the partners is more "Let's see if this feels good to me every day," and the attitude of the other is "I'll be careful, lest he not feel good about me today." The true tragedy is when the more-available sex brings forth a child into this situation. The child usually ends up the product of a never-was but still-broken home.

Notice that at no point did you read, "Couples should not cohabit because it's a sin." As I indicated above, the point is that Christian tradition calls premarital sex and "living together" sinful because they are unhealthy choices that can lead to much unhappiness. When it comes to sex, Catholicism wants people to be happy, to have joy in their lives, and the only way to do that when it comes to sex is to keep it in the context of a healthy marriage where it belongs.

So much for the important side trip. Now back to the main highway. Catholicism insists that sex is a great good and a gift of God, but it "works" the way it is supposed to only in a good marriage. Fine. One trouble is that many of us did grow up in the "old days" of Catholicism with some sexual guilt. Sometimes guilt is perfectly appropriate, but when it comes to sex we got the feeling that sex or sexual feelings should almost always make us feel guilty. This is *not* appropriate.

A cultural reaction to rigid, inappropriate, guilt-inducing attitudes toward sex has been in gear since the 1960s. Unfortunately, this reaction — the so-called "sexual revolution" — took some weird, unhealthy directions. One of the most observable signs of this is the way the entertainment industry presents sex. Movies and television, in particular, trivialize sex, presenting it as just another body function and another recreational activity. Whereas Christianity has always thought of sex as powerful and important, the secular culture's attitudes toward sex are extremely superficial.

So there we are. From the past we may be influenced by a "sex should make you feel guilty" attitude. "If it feels good it must be bad." At the same time, in the present we are influenced by a secular culture that says, "Sex is no big deal; it's like having a good meal or going bowling, only more fun." Catholicism, on the contrary, declares that sex is very good and a big deal, indeed. "There are complex connections between personal sexual identity," writes Christine E. Gudorf in *Body, Sex and Pleasure* (Pilgrim Press, 1994), "and the expression and satisfaction of certain basic physiological and psychological needs and desires. Recognition of the power of sexuality in our lives and world is essential for understanding sexuality as a positive force, as a source of transforming grace."

The attitudes and feelings we have about our sexuality and about the place of sex in marriage have more to do with our spirituality than we may think. Recall Karl Rahner's teaching that we are "embodied spirits." This means that our sexuality and our spirituality are inseparable. We are sexual beings, even spiritually. There is no room — absolutely no room — for either superficiality or inappropriate guilt when it comes to sex. Sex is good, not evil. Sex is important and powerful, not trivial.

Sex is meant to be a source of great joy in marriage. When we trivialize it, joy takes flight. When we make it a source of inappropriate guilt, joy takes flight. Catholicism invites us to keep sex in balance. Sexual pleasure in marriage is a source of grace. It's as simple and profoundly important as that. But there is more to the picture. We can't discuss sex in a Catholic context and avoid the issue of birth control. What do joy, sex, and birth control have to do with one another?

Everyone knows that the Catholic Church's official teaching prohibits the use of artificial contraceptives. Everyone also knows that according to many surveys more than 90 percent of married Catholics believe this prohibition is way off the mark. Unfortunately, too often people make entirely too big a deal out of this.

We are not, after all, talking about an issue that is central to Christian faith. If we look at the big picture of life, death, and the meaning of the universe, birth control is a relatively minor issue. This is not something to throw yourself on your sword about.

If we look at the birth control issue from a cosmic perspective, it turns out to be your basic tempest in a teacup. In spite of all the dust kicked up by those who debate pro and con on birth control, ultimately it comes down to an issue each married couple must deal with, decide about, and live with in peace and joy. It's as basic as that.

There are a few Catholics — almost always of the grim, joyless variety you want to avoid — who act as if God hates people who use artificial contraceptives and is going to damn them to hell for all eternity for doing so. The truth, however, is far more gentle. Ultimately, it comes down to personal conscience, and Catholicism has always taught that we must follow our conscience. St. Augustine said that even if an angel of God should command you to do something contrary to your conscience, you should obey your conscience.

Pope John Paul II has been most insistent that artificial contraceptives are unacceptable. But he, too, is clear about the bottom line. In his international bestseller *Crossing the Threshold of Hope* (Knopf, 1994), John Paul II declares that if a person "is admonished by his [or her] conscience — even if an erroneous conscience, but one whose voice appears to him [or her] as unquestionably true — he [or she] must always listen to it. What is not permissible is that he [or she] culpably indulge in error without trying to reach the truth."

That last sentence simply means that we shouldn't indulge in a mean-spirited avoidance of what is right simply because we get such a charge out of what is clearly wrong. At the same time, it is also true that no one has the right to engage in a mean-spirited condemnation of "so great a cloud of witnesses" (Heb. 12:1) that, in good faith, finds itself in disagreement with the church's official position on birth control. No one can see into another person's heart, conscience, and relationship with God. It's

fine to debate an issue objectively, but there comes a point where
the only Christian thing to do is shut our big mouths and leave
other people and their choices to God.

It is probably true that some married couples choose to use
contraceptives for selfish, joyless reasons. But most do so for the
sake of their marriage and for the sake of the children they already have, for reasons that will increase their joy and their love.
And that is enough.

Catholicism is not about the birth control debate — which
most Catholics no longer debate anyway. Catholicism as it is lived
by the vast majority has bigger fish to fry. The Catholic focus is
primarily on making sense out of life and death, about recogniz-
ing in the life we live the God of Abraham and Sarah, Rebekah
and Isaac, Jacob and Rachel, and Jesus, Mary, and Joseph. The
Catholic focus is on the experience of spiritual healing and liberation (i.e., "salvation"). Church politics and doctrinal squabbles are,
in the long run, peripheral. Although unavoidable in a human,
imperfect church, they are not about the joy at the heart of being
Catholic, and no one should act as if they are.

The Catholic joy of sex is about a woman and a man making love regularly in the context of a healthy marriage. Here's a
true story. A husband and wife — I'll call them Linda and Joe —
had been married for about ten years. They had a son, age seven,
and twin daughters, age five. This couple had enjoyed the sexual
expression of love throughout their marriage, but — a not un-
common phenomenon — only after four years of marriage had
Linda learned to experience orgasm when she and Joe made love.

One Saturday morning, Joe and Linda made love soon after
they woke up, prior to facing another stressful day with their
young children. Linda's orgasm was especially intense, and she
cried out with pleasure, "Jesus, Mary, and Joseph!"

The couple's young son happened to walk by his parents' closed
bedroom door just then, but he continued on downstairs. Later,
he asked his mother, "Mommy, were you praying this morning in
bed?" Linda thought for a moment then said with a smile, "Yes,
I was."

This is the heart of the heart of the matter. The Catholic joy of sex comes from the Catholic experience of sexual pleasure in marriage as a kind of sacrament of the love at the core of the universe. The Letter to the Ephesians calls marriage "a great mystery" (5:32), meaning that it cracks open and reveals the mystery of divine love. That's what the Catholic joy of sex is all about.

CHAPTER SIX

The Joy of the Arts, Poetry, and Stories

Here is a profound mystery, the ultimate mystery of Christian faith: God came into the world in Jesus of Nazareth some two thousand years ago. The doctrinal term for this mystery is "the Incarnation." It means "the embodiment of God in the human form of Jesus." The embodiment of God. God as a human being.

Sit down, sit down. How can we remain standing? We are so familiar with this idea, that God became a human being, that it no longer knocks us over. If we have the slightest inkling of what this means, we are likely to faint dead away. Jesus of Nazareth was fully God and fully human. How can we not fall down with our faces on the ground? How dare we stand up and walk around as if nothing happened out of the ordinary? How can we not stand in awe before every tree, every cloud, every drop of rain, the very sun that filters through the leaves on the trees? If Jesus, the Son of God, walked this earth how can we not kiss the earth?

More than that. If God became human, that makes being human something else altogether. How can we not fall down and worship one another? Or rather, how can we not worship the divine spark in one another? How can we not faint from sheer delight?

More. Jesus the Christ not only lived on this earth, but he died and experienced a transformation we can't begin to understand. We call it "resurrection," but we haven't the slightest idea what that means. We act as if we do, but we do not. Regardless of what it means, however, the most basic result is our experience, for some two thousand years now, of the presence of the risen Christ in the midst of his people. Oh, God. Fall down on the ground with your face to the ground. This is too much, too much, the divine generosity — divine humility, even — behind all this.

Let there be a quiet song. Hum a quiet and holy song without words. Let the music be endless and quiet, for all actions have consequences and this action of the Creator has a profound consequence for all things in time and space. Entering into time and space, in Jesus the Son of God, the Creator makes it lovely for us to draw upon our simple human experience of the divine presence in the world — which is hidden but evident — in order to paint, to write, to build, to draw and sculpt and sing and play upon musical instruments and mold and fashion things both provocative and beautiful.

Because God was — and *is* — embodied in Jesus the Christ, it is good that we express the spirit of our loving intimacy with the risen Christ in the arts, in poetry, and in stories. In the first days of the early Christians, they gathered to pray, they gathered to celebrate their faith, and in Rome sometimes they gathered to bury their martyred dead in tunnels deep in the earth.

Since those early days Catholicism feels compelled, by the spirit of the Incarnation itself, to express its faith in images, words, and music. Through the arts we "incarnate" our experience of the risen Christ and celebrate the Incarnation itself. For some two thousand years now, through the arts we have both expressed and nourished our faith.

Catholicism and Calvinism are polar opposites. Calvinism cries, "God is pure Spirit, not to be captured in visible form! Strip the churches of all decoration! No pictures! No sculpture! No colors! Strip the altar of candles, hang no banners, place no images of the crucified Christ! All such is blasphemy and idolatry!"

Catholicism says, "Don't be silly. God is pure Spirit, but we are not pure spirits, we human beings. Neither is the Son of God pure spirit, then or now. He was fully human and he reigns with a "risen" body. (Whatever that means.) We need sensual ways to nourish our faith and spirituality. We need sacred art, sacred articles, sacred words, and sacred music to help us be in touch with the Son of God who was embodied in the world."

Because Catholicism is sacramental, craving sensuous ways to know and love God, it rejoices in the arts. For what are the arts but sensuous expressions of hidden realities? "Of their nature the arts are directed toward expressing in some way the infinite beauty of God in works made by human hands" (Vatican II, *Constitution on the Sacred Liturgy*, no. 122).

There is great joy in the Catholic appreciation for the arts, for they nourish our spirituality and help us appreciate more deeply how close God is to us, to all of humankind and to the earth. Through images of various kinds and through music we lift heart and soul to God. Like the Gospel, however, the purpose of the arts is not only to comfort and uplift, but to challenge us to grow as well.

We are a cushy lot, we North Americans on the verge of a new century. We want life to be predictable. Political conservatism is popular. Conservative perspectives on religion are popular. In such a time it may be the task of the artist to shake us up. The artist should sometimes produce work that challenges the status quo — a painting, some music, a poem, a story, or a piece of sculpture that hits us right between the eyes with some truth we would rather not think about.

Imagine, for example, a crucifix. But imagine also that the body on the crucifix is not male but female. Perhaps this shocks you to your toes. Perhaps you are scandalized to see the dead body of a young woman on a cross. Her full breasts. Her beautiful figure. Dead. Perhaps you are offended and indignant. But perhaps, if you are honest with yourself, you are also a tiny bit intrigued. Jesus was a man, it's true. But this is an example of art meant not to comfort and/or inspire, but to make us think — perhaps even call us to repentance and conversion of heart.

As we gaze at the female figure on the cross, unless we protect ourselves by becoming merely indignant, unless we deny the right of the artist to challenge us, we must ask ourselves some questions. What is the meaning of the female body to me? What is the meaning of the male body to me? To our culture? To Catholicism? Why am I shocked and offended by a crucifix with a female figure on it? Why am I a little bit intrigued?

By entering into dialogue with questions such as these, I may find an unexpected joy. A small revelation. Perhaps I look at a painting of the Blessed Virgin Mary that rejects traditional Marian imagery. Perhaps this is a cosmic Virgin, a small smile on her lips, her face showing great peace, her breasts bared, a crown of stars around her head, floating in a dark, royal blue sky filled with stars. How do I feel about such a painting? Why? There is joy available through art, for it draws us "to adoration, to prayer, and to the love of God, Creator and Savior, the Holy One and Sanctifier" (*Catechism of the Catholic Church*, no. 2502).

One of the hallmarks of Catholicism is its capacity to find truth, beauty, and goodness — and therefore joy — lurking almost anyplace. A work of art need have no explicitly religious character in order to reveal the sacred. We may find sacred truth in John Steinbeck's *The Grapes of Wrath* as easily as in Dante's *Divine Comedy*. We may discover the holy in a song by a popular rock group as easily as in Gregorian chant.

There is no more obvious illustration of the Catholic love for art than a great many parish churches. In Catholic churches you will find statues — some in bad taste, it's true, but one may develop an affection even for these. You will find at least one crucifix in one style or another. Bas-relief, painted, or abstract Stations of the Cross decorate the walls. Stained glass fills the windows. Statues of saints and angels may be there. The interior of the church appeals to the soul through the senses. Even newer Catholic churches will have a statue of Mary and perhaps St. Joseph, for in such images there is joy. One must admit, unfortunately, that some new Catholic churches lean more in the direction of Calvinism's rejection of images and art than in the direction of the living Catholic tradition. God willing, with time balance will return.

The Second Vatican Council declared that church interiors should avoid "sumptuous display" and any art that might "offend true religious sense either by depraved forms or through lack of artistic merit or because of mediocrity or pretense." At the same time, the council said that "the placing of sacred images in churches...is to be maintained," but "their number should be moderate and their relative positions should reflect right order." Otherwise, people might "find them incongruous and they may foster devotion of doubtful orthodoxy" (*Constitution on the Sacred Liturgy*, nos. 124–25).

Lord knows.

All the same, images and art belong in Catholic churches for the joy they give through the reminders they offer. Still, enough is enough for heaven's sake, so avoid so-called art that makes you want to say, "Blecch." There is an abundance of such "art" floating around in Catholic circles. No joy, except in the good-natured chuckles it is likely to inspire. What can one do? When you're talking about the oldest institution in the Western world, you need to allow for some bizarre things that crept in along the way. A sense of humor helps.

The Swiss Catholic philosopher Max Picard (1888–1965) wrote a book called *The World of Silence* (Regnery/Gateway, 1952). Among his meditations, Picard included a brief chapter "Images and Silence," and the Catholic joy in images comes through clearly on every page.

"Images are silent," Picard wrote, "but they speak in silence. They are a silent language." Images, whether in paintings, statues, stained glass, or another medium fill the great cathedrals of Europe. In France alone, Notre Dame, Chartres, St. Denis, and Mont St. Michel are but four of the best known. In preliterate cultures, the people "heard" the Good News through images that "spoke" a language of their own, a "silent language."

"Images and pictures," Max Picard explained, remind us "of life before the coming of language"; they move us "with a yearning for that life." For the human soul, unlike the mind, does not express itself through words but through images. Thus, to spend time with images and pictures is to expose the soul to a deep source of life and joy.

Today, sad to say, we are bombarded by images from the mass media, everything from television to billboards, from magazines to movies. We experience the power of images, but so heavy is the commercial and secular bombardment that we become desensitized and find it difficult to respond. We become "nervous and confused," Picard said, "because the images whose real nature it is to create peace in the soul bring...an uneasy lack of peace instead." This is what happens when images are used for a base purpose. "The images no longer give the peace of their own silence to the soul; they take peace from the soul by disturbing and consuming it with their riotous jostling with one another."

Thus, when we do stand before genuinely artistic images, rather than images thrown at us for commercial purposes, we may need to make extra effort to be open to the power of the good image. There is joy in images that originate in the soul of the artist, darkness and despair in images that originate in the lust for corporate profits. Catholicism would punctuate life with images that, like the Gospel, comfort the afflicted, who are all of us, and afflict the comfortable, who are all of us. In both cases, the result would be a more joyful heart.

Writing is an art, too, including poetry, fiction, drama, and nonfiction. Catholicism's love for the written word is intense and sometimes startling. Only a Catholic writer — in this case the English Jesuit Gerard Manley Hopkins (1844–89) — could write a poem like this, which he called "God's Grandeur":

> The world is charged with the beauty of God.
> It will flame out, like shining from shook foil;
> It gathers to a greatness, like the ooze of oil
> Crushed. Why do men then now not reck his rod?
> Generations have trod, have trod, have trod;
> And all is seared with trade; bleared, smeared with toil;
> And wears man's smudges and shares man's smell: the soil
> Is bare now, nor can foot feel, being shod.

And for all that, nature is never spent;
There lives the dearest freshness deep down things:
And through the last lights off the black West went
Oh, morning, at the brown brink eastward, springs —
Because the Holy Ghost over the bent
World broods with warm breast and with ah! bright wings.

Notice the depth of Hopkins's appreciation for the holiness of the earth. Because he was Catholic, all of Creation was for him an analogy for God, even a kind of sacrament. Thomas Merton (1915–68), who was a Trappist monk, author and poet, and perhaps the most prominent American Catholic of the twentieth century, wrote something similar. He wrote: "Life is this simple: We are living in a transparent world, and God shines through in every moment. This is not just a fable or a nice story; it is a living truth... God manifests everywhere, in everything. We cannot be without God. It's impossible. It's simply impossible."

The American Catholic short story writer Flannery O'Connor (1925–64) was the first woman to have her work published in the prestigious Library of America series. Her stories and letters reveal a profoundly sacramental view of life and the world. Weird as her characters and story lines frequently are, they nevertheless break open the holy mystery at the heart of the created order. Indeed, O'Connor's primary purpose in writing stories was to expose dimensions of religious mystery that threaten the status quo. In a story called "Greenleaf," for example, O'Connor wrote:

> She continued to stare straight ahead but the entire scene in front of her had changed — the tree line was an open wound in a world that was nothing but sky — and she had the look of a person whose sight had been suddenly restored but who finds the light unbearable.

In a posthumous collection of letters, *The Habit of Being*, edited by Sally Fitzgerald (Farrar, Straus & Giroux, 1979), Flannery O'Connor explains the irony of her situation as a Catholic writer in words that should capture the attention of anyone frustrated or disillusioned with the Catholic Church:

> I write the way I do because (not though) I am a Catholic. This is a fact and nothing covers it like the bald statement. However, I am a Catholic peculiarly possessed of the modern consciousness, that thing Jung describes as unhistorical, solitary, and guilty. To possess this *within* the Church is to bear a burden, the necessary burden for the conscious Catholic. It's to feel the contemporary situation at the ultimate level. I think that the Church is the only thing that is going to make the terrible world we are coming to endurable; the only thing that makes the Church endurable is that it is somehow the body of Christ and that on this we are fed. It seems to be a fact that you have to suffer as much from the Church as for it but if you believe in the divinity of Christ, you have to cherish the world at the same time that you struggle to endure it.

Flannery O'Connor was Catholic to her bones, but she insisted that a Catholic worships God, not the church, and certainly not church institutions. In 1962, O'Connor wrote a review of a biography of Cardinal Francis Spellman, then the archbishop of New York. In this review O'Connor deflated the cardinal — and clerical windbags in general — with a gift for the written word much to be admired:

> We are given many official letters and telegrams verbatim and sizable portions of the Cardinal's sermons. Cardinal Spellman has apparently often given as many as seven talks a day, a feat which would kill a lesser man, but which must account for the ease with which he exercises the clerical gift for bringing forth the sonorous familiar phrase of slowly deadening effect.

Another contemporary Catholic writer, Walker Percy (1916–90), also felt both alienated from the world and united with the deepest mystery at the heart of the world. In *The Message in the Bottle* (Farrar, Straus & Giroux, 1975), he wrote:

> The Christian novelist nowadays is like a man who has found a treasure hidden in the attic of an old house, but he is writing for people who have moved out to the suburbs and who are bloody sick of the old house and everything in it.

What Walker Percy said about the Christian novelist is true not just for novelists. Believers of many stripes find themselves living in the attic of an old house — the church — that many people are no longer interested in. They are "bloody sick of the old house and everything in it." This is the challenge. What do we do about this? To sit here in our attic and take on an attitude of smug superiority will not do. This is the dilemma writers such as Walker Percy and Flannery O'Connor confront us with through their stories. This is what we might call the "prophetic" function of the artist.

Other Catholic writers, while not denying the reality of this dilemma, write stories in which genuine faith is woven into the fabric of their fictional characters' lives. James Lee Burke, for example, is a Catholic writer of popular and highly literary crime fiction. His character Dave Robicheaux is a Louisiana Cajun Catholic, a recovering alcoholic, and sometime police detective. In an early Dave Robicheaux novel, *Heaven's Prisoners* (Henry Holt, 1988), Dave rescues a little Salvadoran girl from a plane crash in a swamp near his home, a crash in which the girl's mother is killed. The little girl — whom Dave named Alafair — asks in Spanish where her mother is, so Dave and his wife, Annie, respond from an honest faith perspective:

> So we drove her to St. Peter's Church in New Iberia. I suppose one might say that my attempt at resolution was facile. But I believe that ritual and metaphor exist for a reason.... We each held her hand and walked her up the aisle of the empty church to the scrolled metal stand of

burning candles that stood before statues of Mary, Joseph, and the infant Jesus.

"*Ta maman est avec Jésus,*" I said to her in French. "*Au ciel.*"

Her face was round, and her eyes blinked at me.

"*Cielo?*" she asked.

"Yes, in the sky. *Au ciel,*" I said.

"*En el cielo,*" Annie said. "In heaven."

Alafair's face was perplexed as she at first looked back and forth between us, then I saw her lips purse and her eyes start to water.

"Hey, hey, little guy," I said, and picked her up on my hip. "Come on, I want you to light a candle. *Pour ta maman.*"

I lit the punk on a burning candle, put it in her hand, and helped her touch it to a dead wick inside a red glass candle container.

André Dubus is another Catholic fiction author. Mostly a writer of powerful short stories, in a rare novel, *Voices from the Moon* (David R. Godine, 1984), Dubus ends his story with words that reveal a sacramental sensitivity to rival that of the poet Hopkins:

> What he felt was the night air starting to cool, and the dew on the grass under his hand holding Melissa's, and under his arms and head and shirt, and only its coolness touching his thick jeans, and the heels of his shoes. He felt Melissa's hand in his, and the beating of his heart as she both quickened and soothed, and he smelled the length of her beside him, and heard in the trees the song of cicadas like the distant ringing of a thousand tambourines. He saw in the stars the eyes of God too, and was grateful for them, as he was for the night and the girl he loved. He lay on the grass and the soft summer earth, holding Melissa's hand, and talking to the stars.

Other contemporary Catholic fiction writers that belong on any list are Jon Hassler, Mary Higgins Clark, Andrew M.

Greeley, J. F. Powers, Annie Dillard, and Ron Hansen. If you read their stories you will find their Catholic sensibilities on every page.

It is the privilege of the story-teller, like any artist, to speak of "things invisible to see" (the phrase is from seventeenth-century English poet John Donne) using as metaphors things we see quite plainly every day. It is one of the joys of being Catholic to read such stories and be able to connect with the metaphors and analogies we find there not just on an aesthetic level but on a faith level, on the level of one's personal experience of the Divine Mystery.

Catholic novelist Ron Hansen said it well in an article published in *Image*, "A Journal of the Arts and Religion": "Writing ... is a sacrament insofar as it provides graced occasions of encounter between humanity and God.... The job of fiction writers is to fashion ... symbols and give their readers the feeling that life has great significance, that something is going on here that matters."

Now it must be said that in the end — from a Catholic point of view, at least — there can be no division between religious and secular art. "Basically," said Madeleine L'Engle in *Walking On Water* (Harold Shaw, 1980), "there can be no categories such as 'religious' art and 'secular' art, because all true art is incarnational, and therefore 'religious.'"

It is just as possible to find religious meaning in a work by an artist who claims to be an agnostic or atheist as in a work by someone who claims religious identity. This is one of the joys of being Catholic, to find meaning, truth, and beauty wherever they happen to percolate. If anything, the Catholic sacramental imagination will find *more* meaning, truth, and beauty in works of art than do others. Being Catholic inclines the heart that way.

Coming full-circle, back to poetry, a Catholic can pick up American poet Robert Wrigley's collection *In the Bank of Beautiful Sins* (Penguin Books, 1995) and revel in the poet's images and metaphors. Wrigley belongs in Walker Percy's metaphor, one of those who are "bloody sick of the old house," organized religion. "I've never trusted church-bound religion," Wrigley told an interviewer, "but I love faith. Poetry is my religion. The act of writing is the closest I can come to prayer."

Robert Wrigley's poems reflect a highly tuned sensitivity to human and spiritual concerns. His writing taps into our lives and awakens us to a deeper awareness of what goes on there, echoing the feelings, thoughts, and experiences of an authentic spiritual seeker. "I love ambiguity," he says; "it opens up possibilities."

Authentic Catholicism finds a deep and quiet joy in the work of such a poet. Its honesty is prophetic, cracking the whip above our heads, snapping us to attention, saying, look here: religion should never, never, never be an escape clause, and shame on those who lead others to think that religion is boring. Poets such as Robert Wrigley help us to remember that an honest atheist is preferable to a phony believer. In Wrigley's words, "salvation is an enterprise, grace the bottom line." Always, in this world, salvation is an enterprise and grace is the bottom line.

In his poem "The Nothing-God," Robert Wrigley paints an understated but shocking portrait of a girl abused by her father. Where, Wrigley seems to ask, is God in this horrible experience? In this situation one can find only a "nothing-god." The final section of the poem says:

> She's saying her name now, a single up-sung complaint,
> like the call of a mournful bird, and when
> his truck grinds down the steep trail to the shack,
> she'll feel that shimmering fog return to her —
> the nothing-god, allowing this world to happen
> nightly, again and again, every mark on her
> instantly numb, the nothing-god,
> the soul of ice, and winter, winter coming on.

Is our God sometimes a "nothing-god"? Is there some kinship between this and the Western mystical tradition of a "dark night of the soul"? If so, what is it? If not, then do not look away, do not pretend that some fathers do not abuse their daughters. What does your God say about this? Do not look away. Do not try to turn your religion into an escape clause or mere security blanket.

Do not. Look, and wait, and keep your eyes open, and feel the pain, and face the question. Even if no answer seems to be forthcoming. Especially then. That is one message of a poem such as this one.

Robert Wrigley is no church-person, but Catholicism loves his honesty and his affection for ambiguity that liberates him, and us, from the worship of false gods. At the same time, Catholicism takes joy in the work of other poets who sing of the goodness and beauty in people and in God's Creation. The later poetry, especially, of Mark Van Doren (1894–1972) thrills the heart with its uninhibited affection for the glory of being alive.

In Van Doren's last collection of poems, *Good Morning* (Hill and Wang, 1973), there is a poem called "And All the While." The poet reflects on the mystery that grounds his own being:

> And all the while,
> Down under,
> Something lives
> That I can't see,
> Though it is mine,
> Though it is me.
>
> Without me here
> It wouldn't be there;
> But neither could I
> Be more than I am —
> Which is what I desire —
> Were I wholly alone.
>
> I must not try
> Too hard or too long,
> Or even at all,
> To guess what it is:
> So ancient, so still,
> So known and unknown.

In an earlier book, *That Shining Place* (Hill and Wang, 1969), Mark Van Doren included eleven "Psalms" that echo beautifully the poet's marvelous but institutionally disconnected faith. One of the shortest, and perhaps the most touching, is Psalm 2:

> He sings to me when I am sad.
> His voice is old, but sweeter than new honey.
> It comes from farther off than I can see.
> It is not the world singing, it is he
> That made it, and he makes it once again
> As way down here I listen,
> Listen, and am sad once more
> With so much sweetness,
> Sweetness — O, my Lord, how can I bear it?
> Yet bear it, says the song, and so I do,
> I bear it, all that sweetness, as he has
> Forever, says the song he sings to me.

Art — of word, image, or music — is incarnational; it carries something bigger than itself. It sings or whistles and takes us by the hand or the heart and skips us along paths we might not otherwise take. Along those paths we discover new insights into ourselves, into life and the world, yes, but more than that. Along those paths we discover the Divine Mystery itself, and in that discovery there is, in the end, joy not to be described. That is why artists — believers, unbelievers, and "in-betweeners" — are so important to Catholicism.

In the best of all possible worlds, where we would find the best of all possible churches, the Catholic Church would be so faithful to its own spirit and its own deepest truth that no artist would be able to resist Catholicism, so deep is its affection for the arts. Now and then, an artist is able to see past the church's inevitable sins, foolishness, and short-sightedness and embrace it all the same. Now and then, an artist is able to forgive the church and love it all the same. This happened, for example, in the case of the writers Walker Percy and Annie Dillard, who converted to Catholicism. Now and then this happens, and in Annie Dillard's case it happened, in part at least, because she had the capacity to both love and laugh. In *Teaching a Stone to Talk* (Harper & Row, 1982), she wrote about her experience attending Mass:

> During the long intercessory prayer, the priest always reads "intentions" from the parishioners. These are slips of paper, dropped into a box before the service begins, on which people have written their private concerns ... and we respond on cue. "For a baby safely delivered on November twentieth," the priest intoned, "we pray to the Lord." We all responded, "Lord, hear our prayer." Suddenly the priest broke in and confided to our bowed heads, "That's the baby we've been praying for the past two months! The woman just kept getting more and more pregnant!" How often, how shockingly often, have I exhausted myself in church from the effort to keep from laughing out loud? I often laugh all the way home.

Annie Dillard reminds us that sometimes when it comes to the church our salvation is in laughter. Sometimes we, the church, take ourselves *so seriously*. Sometimes the church's leaders at any level act in ways that would turn us grim, grim, grim, unless we allow ourselves to see how ludicrous it all is ... and allow ourselves to laugh right out loud. If we notice things getting *serious*, often if we listen carefully to the music of the stars at night, we will hear the Voice of God saying: "Lighten up, people!" Sometimes there is great freedom and love in laughing all the way home.

But back to the main theme: In its heart of hearts Catholicism takes great joy in the arts, in poetry, in stories, and in music, for they sing and speak of the Divine Mystery in ways nothing else can. Catholicism finds joy in the arts because the arts carry us right into the Divine Mystery, and when we find ourselves there we find ourselves swimming in a mysterious Love.

Chapter Seven

The Joy of the Intellectual Life

A young university professor was on his way to teach an extension course in a rural community. Occupying an aisle seat in a small commuter jet aircraft, he read and took notes for the lecture he would give that evening on twentieth-century New Testament scholarship.

From the seat across the aisle came the hand of a middle-aged man holding a small card, which he obviously wanted the young professor to take and read. Printed on the card were these words: "Abandon the vanities of the mind and accept the Lord Jesus as your Personal Savior."

The young professor handed the card back, smiled politely, and said nothing. What he wanted to say was: "God gave you a brain and you're expected to use it." The intellect clearly has its limits, but who can believe that faith requires us to stop thinking? The concept of "blind faith" is un-Christian in the extreme.

Catholicism takes particular joy in the intellectual life. So do not underestimate the place of the intellect in the life of faith. From the first-century writers and redactors of the various divinely inspired New Testament documents down to our own time, believers have felt compelled to *think about* their faith, to try to better understand its implications for various historical and cultural settings.

Catholicism holds some of its intellectuals in such high regard that it awards them the title "Doctor of the Church." Note in passing an astonishing fact. A thinker's work need not be free from error in all respects in order for him or her to be named a Doctor of the Church. Consider the implications, if you will. This suggests that Catholic intellectuals have the freedom to pursue their research and be creative, to examine even ideas that may seem to threaten the faith or lead to a cognitive dead end. Indeed, there is more than enough room for disagreement among Catholic intellectuals and even between intellectuals and the church's official authorities.

In fact, there is nothing new about this. Even the various New Testament documents sometimes present conflicting points of view. In the Gospel of Mark, for example, on the question of divorce Jesus makes an unqualified statement: "Whoever divorces his wife and marries another commits adultery against her; and if she divorces her husband and marries another, she commits adultery" (10:11–12). Period. No exceptions. In Matthew, however, Jesus clearly allows for exceptions to the rule: "But I say to you that anyone who divorces his wife, *except on the ground of unchastity,* causes her to commit adultery" (5:32; emphasis added).

The faith experience from which Matthew's Gospel comes saw the necessity to modify the absolute prohibition articulated by Jesus in Mark's Gospel, which was written earlier. If one exception is possible, other exceptions are possible.

If an intellectual can make a few mistakes and still be named a Doctor of the Church, he or she may feel free to follow the dictates of conscience in the intellectual life. More than a few Catholic intellectuals are encouraged by the fact that, in the past, some thinkers were silenced by church authorities only to be celebrated later as great theologians who made tremendous contributions to the church's self-understanding.

The most recently named Doctors of the Church are St. Catherine of Siena (1347–80) and St. Teresa of Avila (1515–82). Both received the title in 1970. Not without significance is the fact that both are women.

The Letters of Paul clearly illustrate the high regard in which the author held the human intellect. All one need do is sit down and read the Letter to the Romans to see how important Paul believed it is to bring the powers of the intellect to bear on the life of faith. The early "fathers of the church" — including Ignatius of Antioch, Tertullian, and Polycarp — were intellectual giants of their time. St. Augustine, in the fifth century, wrote books still considered major classics of world literature. These include his *Confessions* — the first book ever written in the first person — and *The City of God.*

Some of the greatest saints of the church were intellectuals. St. Anselm, in the eleventh century, was the first to incorporate successfully the rationalism of Aristotelian dialectics into Christian theology. Anselm's definition of theology remains valid some nine centuries after he wrote it: "Faith in search of understanding."

Many would say that the greatest intellectual in the history of Catholicism was St. Thomas Aquinas (1225–74), whose theological writings — in particular, his *Summa theologiae* — have had a profound impact on theologians down to our own time. Thomas insisted that faith and reason are not in conflict; rather, they are meant to complete each other. Reason finds its natural fulfillment in faith, yet reason left to itself can establish divine truths such as the existence of God.

This is where the joy of the intellectual life comes from, the search to better understand God's love and the ongoing presence of the risen Christ in our midst. There is joy in ideas, in trying to think things out, in trying to put two and two together, in struggling to overcome intellectual obstacles, in trying to come up with solutions to problems. There is joy in using the brains God gave us, in developing theories and hypotheses that attempt to apply the basic Gospel message to the realities of modern life. Indeed, the intellectual life is sometimes compared to a game. There is a kind of playfulness to it that Catholicism cherishes.

And yet... it is also true that among modern North American Catholics, in particular, the intellectual life has trouble getting much respect. In the early 1970s, a weighty tome entitled *Christ Sein* (English title, *On Being a Christian*), by theologian Hans

Küng, remained on the bestseller lists in Germany for months. In the United States, the book sold moderately well in religious circles, but it hadn't a ghost of a chance to become a bestseller. Something there is about Americans that does not appreciate the life of the intellect, particularly when it comes to religion. A great American, Thomas Edison, once said that most people would rather die than think.

Catholicism has an illustrious intellectual tradition, but it has yet to catch on in the United States. Indeed, time was popular Catholic spiritual guides actually discouraged the intellectual life. Many a Catholic who grew up in the 1930s, '40s, and '50s can recall having lines quoted at them from *The Imitation of Christ,* a book often called the most widely read book in the world, after the Bible. The lines go like this: "I would rather be able to feel compunction [i.e., regret for past misdeeds] in my heart than be able to define it." And: "Learned arguments do not make a man holy."

The piety of an earlier generation scorned "intellectualism" as dangerous to the spiritual life. But those who quoted this line approvingly overlooked something a bit of research would have shown them. The fifteenth-century author of *The Imitation of Christ,* Thomas à Kempis, who lived in the Netherlands, belonged to a group called the Brethren of the Common Life. He had been trained in what was called the *Devotio Moderna,* a spirituality that placed great value on the intellect and academic studies. In other words, Thomas à Kempis *took for granted* the goodness and value of intellectual pursuits while cautioning the reader against intellectual activities divorced from the love of God and neighbor. The last thing Thomas would want to do is place the intellectual life in a negative light.

Many Catholics who grew up during roughly the first half of this century recall learning the basics of their faith from the *Baltimore Catechism.* This venerable volume presented the current understanding of Catholicism in a series of 299 questions and answers, which children were expected to memorize. In other words, it appealed almost entirely to the intellect. Yet the old catechism did not encourage children to appreciate the intellectual life. Once you had all the answers memorized that was all the thinking you needed to do. For the remainder of your life you had your faith all tied up in a neat little package. Thus, many adult Catholics today see no reason to spend much time learning more about their faith. They may be highly educated in other respects, but when it comes to their religion they miss out on the joy of the intellectual life.

Not that subsequent generations of Catholics have been encouraged to think about their faith either. Since the mid-1960s, an emphasis in catechetics on "feelings" and "experience" leaves many younger adult Catholics with little of a cognitive nature to rely upon when it comes to their religion. Many of them couldn't say anything rational about sacraments, for example, if their lives depended on it.

Of course, the cultural context is no help. We live in a culture some call "postliterate." Television and other forms of video have a stranglehold on the popular mind. So how likely is the average person to pick up a book — particularly one filled with religious *ideas* — and read it? Even college-educated Catholics often miss out on the joys of the intellectual life, never having experienced, even in college, the pleasures of the intellect.

Let us launch a small exploration, a minor adventure, if you will. Let us speculate about the connections between the intellect and spirituality. Quietly, now, let's sneak up on the topic, catch it by surprise, and see what it may toss into the air . . .

First, we pose a question: What do we mean by "spirituality"? Let us suppose that by this word we mean the ways a person tries consciously to live his or her life in relation to the Divine Mystery, God, the Ground of All Being, the Great Cosmic Wherewithal. Whatever. So spirituality would be closely related to that fuzzy-wuzzy concept, "lifestyle." However we go about living, including the values and goals we choose, is also how we go about our spirituality. We're not talking only about prayer and other "spiritual exercises" here, although these are part of a person's lifestyle and spirituality.

Now let's sharpen the focus still more. What do we mean by "Christian spirituality" specifically? What makes spirituality distinctively Christian? In this case, the idea is not only to live in conscious relation to God, but to do so in the context of an explicitly Christian faith, meaning conscious relation to the risen Christ who lives in the midst of his people, the church...and everyplace else, too, for that matter.

Living in conscious relation to the risen Christ and being open to his presence in every dimension of daily life, this is what makes a Christian spirituality and lifestyle unique. But what about a spirituality and lifestyle that are not only Christian but *Catholic?* In this case, a person's spirituality becomes explicitly *sacramental* and *incarnational.* In other words, for a Catholic living in relation to the risen Christ is a project that cherishes sensuous ways to know and experience God's love. Love of God and neighbor become inseparable. A Catholic cherishes liturgical forms of worship because they appeal to the senses. A Catholic cherishes all of Creation — sunsets and insects, trees and lemons, leaping dogs and quiet cats, breathing in and breathing out — because all of Creation is in the Creator and reflects the goodness and wonder of God's love.

This being the case, where does the intellectual life fit into such a spirituality and lifestyle? It fits like a hand in a glove. For the intellect, too, is sacramental, a part of Creation that can beat the Holy of Holies out of the bushes. Now and then. Here and there. Time and again. Here is where the intellectual life belongs, as a way to swim around in the ocean of thought and sometimes feel the ecstasy of basking in the light, sometimes feel the confusion of stumbling in the dark. Both are sacraments of communion with the risen Christ who came into the world with a human intellect. If it was good enough for him, it's good enough for us. He used his noodle, he thought things out, and so should we.

Let's say that we have not exercised the old gray matter much in recent years. So how can we begin to include the intellectual life in our spirituality? The game's afoot, but how do we join in?

No problem. Piece of cake. Where do your natural questions lead you? Let your mind do the walking. Are you intrigued by the Bible? Always had some curiosity about the Scriptures that you have done nothing about? Until now? Excellent. Time to ratchet up your natural curiosity about the Bible and let it work for you, give you some joy.

Lay your hands on a good modern translation of the Bible, of course. Can't do better than the New Revised Standard Version or the New American Bible with Revised New Testament. Best translations going. Avoid paraphrases (e.g., *The Living Bible*) if what you want is understanding, if what you want is what's in the Bible, not one man's pious opinion of what's in the Bible.

Then — and here's where our intellectual wings lift us into the air — lay your hands on a couple of books *about* the Bible. Highly recommended: *Responses to 101 Questions on the Bible*, by Raymond E. Brown (Paulist Press, 1990). Father Brown will knock your socks off. Great place to start *thinking about* the Bible. Read it and hang on to your socks.

Say you want something of a more general nature. And maybe you are ready to read around, dip in here and there, now and then. Maybe you want to look at Catholicism, think about Catholicism, at random and at your leisure, but you want to tackle a heavy hitter. Relatively speaking. The *Catechism of the Catholic Church* (many different publishers, you can find it just about anywhere) covers all the basics from the official point of view. *Catholicism*, revised edition, by Richard P. McBrien (HarperSan-Francisco, 1994) is a resource to dip into, read around in, for the neophyte or the veteran intellectual. Super.

Say you want to start out general but with a lighter touch. Lay your hands on *The People's Catechism*, edited by Raymond A. Lucker, et al. (Crossroad Publishing Co., 1995). Here you get thoughts to think over spiced with stories that both entertain and inform. Also you get suggestions for working the ideas into your lifestyle and spirituality.

Catholics find joy in the intellectual life that sometimes spills over into quiet ecstasy. Why? Because to use the intellect is to do something no other creature on the earth can do. To use the intellect is to exercise our humanity in wondrous ways. Let us, then whet our intellectual appetite. Let us do this by dipping into some of the actual thoughts of some modern Catholic intellectual superstars. Celebrity thinkers, if you will. Let us sit on the edge of the pool and wiggle our toes in the water. We will not try to tackle their highly technical stuff, of course; that's for professional theologians and students of theology. We will look at what they say to all of us. Perhaps this will tempt us to throw caution to the wind and jump in ourselves.

Karl Rahner

Many would agree that Karl Rahner, S.J. (1904–84), was the greatest Catholic theologian of the twentieth century. The German Jesuit's technical writings are difficult to penetrate, yet the implications of his ideas are both faithful to the deepest and best in Catholicism and at the same time spiritually liberating in the extreme. Rahner wrote about the most abstruse theological problems and the most homely everyday issues. To read Rahner is to have a most delightful adventure of the intellect and soul.

Yet Rahner also wrote small, simple — one might almost say pious — books, as well, that were based upon his theology. Let us consider two of his thoughts geared to a more popular audience, from his little book, *Words of Faith* (Crossroad Publishing Co., 1987):

GENUINE CHRISTIANS

When God speaks to us and calls us, and we do the work of faith throughout our lives, and if we really love God and our neighbor through this faith — do not merely feel an emotion but love them in actual deeds of sacrifice — and if we are steadfast in hope because we know that we are pilgrims and that ultimate reality still lies ahead, if we practice this self-sacrificing love, active faith, and unshakable hope — then we are genuine Christians. In the divine Spirit that is poured forth in our hearts, we shall then be able to endure joyfully the afflictions, the bitterness, the difficulties, the trials of our lives, of which Christians have not less but more than other people. For the Christian is a strange kind of person who simultaneously experiences tribulation and the joy of the Holy Spirit, which is deeper and more penetrating than any tribulation; joy that is strong and active and endures unto the end.

Pay close attention to these deceptively quiet words of the great theologian, for they are loaded with dynamite. Notice. Rahner insists that love is not merely an emotion. Dynamite. We live in a world that believes in love as nothing *but* an emotion. If you don't "feel" love, then it doesn't exist. An unpopular notion, that love should require "deeds of sacrifice." Yes, this is the heart of the matter, Rahner says. "Sacrificing love." No marriage, no friendship, no vocation to any way of life can survive without it.

And what's this? Christians, Rahner says, have not fewer but more difficulties in life than other people. Just what we needed to hear! But that's not the ultimate point, Rahner adds. The ultimate reality for a Christian — and the focus of this book — is that we have a joy far deeper and more real than any suffering life may send our way.

OUR LIFE'S GREAT WORK

This is our life's great work: to accept ourselves as the mysterious and gradually revealed gift of the eternal generosity of God. For everything that we are and have, even the painful and mysterious, is God's generous gift; we must not grumble at it but must accept it in the knowledge that when we do so God gives himself with his gift and so gives us everything that we could receive. To do this is the wisdom and the chief work of a Christian life. If we look into our own lives we will find that we have not always done it.

All of us, young and old alike, are really latecomers. And yet God is willing to give us everything if we will only accept it — ourselves and himself and life without end.

What can this mean? That the most important task we have in life is to "accept ourselves"? Yes! When we get down to essentials, what is more difficult in the long run and sometimes in the short run? Yet this is what we are to do, accept ourselves, because to accept ourselves is to accept God and God's will for us. We work for a lifetime at saying: I accept myself as "the mysterious, gradually revealed gift of the eternal generosity of God."

And how do we do this? We accept ourselves by accepting the need to work through the dark as well as rejoice in the light. We accept ourselves by saying "yes" to the consequences of the choices we make, pleasant or unpleasant. For when we accept ourselves we accept God's eternally loving presence in ourselves.

Talk about a wonderful blessing and a wonderful mystery....

Monika Hellwig

One of the most articulate and perceptive American theologians of our time, Monika Hellwig is a single, adoptive mother of two children (now grown), a professor of theology at Georgetown University, and the author of more than a dozen books. In *What Are the Theologians Saying Now?* (Christian Classics, 1992) Monika Hellwig provides an excellent, concise overview of major theological trends since the mid-1960s. Here is one thought-provoking excerpt:

THE CHURCH IS ALWAYS BEHIND

The questions that arise from today's world and experience will reach the experts tomorrow. When the moral theologians or the systematic theologians understand the dimensions of the question, they will want to turn to the work of biblical scholars to find out what resources Scripture may offer for the solution, and to patrologists for resources in the early history of the church, as well as to historians, canonists and other experts. All of this takes time. If the solutions proposed converge, it will still take time for them to gain the status of church teachings. If they do not converge and authority must intervene explicitly, that will certainly take much longer again. The result of such inevitable delays is that official teaching is often addressing past problems and questions, while new questions are those which really concern the faithful of the time. Continued development and change is what we must expect.

What's this? Monika Hellwig explains that the Catholic Church's theologians and official teachers are likely to be playing catch-up most of the time. A delightful perspective! Sometimes our leaders lead by following. Rejoice! One may add that sometimes — maybe much of the time — they don't seem aware that this is what they are doing. Nobody's perfect.

Of course, this doesn't mean that we, the people, know it all. It simply means that we, all of us together, people and leaders, *experience* the cutting edge of the life of faith all the time, and the church's official leaders and theologians do their best to help us understand, in retrospect, what is going on. Or was going on. In the process everyone makes mistakes. We all do the best we can. The love of God is always and everywhere dependable and unconditional. It's as simple as that.

Raymond E. Brown

The greatest American Catholic biblical scholar of our time, the earlier mentioned Father Raymond E. Brown, is the kind of scholar whose writings irritate conservative Catholics one moment, then perplex liberal Catholics the next. This is a tip-off that in Father Brown's writings you will find the work of a scholar who both loves the church and believes that Catholicism has nothing to fear from the truth.

In *Responses to 101 Questions on the Bible* (Paulist Press, 1990), Father Raymond Brown offers perhaps the best brief introduction available for the average reader on the Catholic perspective on reading and interpreting the Bible. In response to a question about whether the Gospels are biographies of Jesus or not, Father Brown says in part:

> While in general the Gospels are not biographies, the Gospel According to Luke, since it is joined to the Book of Acts, which narrates a loose type of history of the early Christians, and since it does have a story of Jesus' conception, birth, and youth, would come closer to the appearance of a biography than any of the other Gospels. Also, while no Gospel gives us a complete or dispassionate account of Jesus' life, all the Gospels give us some historical data about the circumstances of his life, his words, and his deeds. Therefore the statement that the Gospels are not biographies does not in any way rule out that their portraits are more than simply theological evaluations — they are interpretations of a real life, real words, and real deeds.

Some Christians, including some Catholics, have fits insisting that the Gospels record exactly what Jesus said and did, as if eyewitnesses wrote down everything. The official teaching of the Catholic Church declares, on the contrary, that the Gospels developed in three stages: the stage of the historical Jesus, the stage of the oral tradition that followed the death and resurrection of Jesus, and the phase during which the Gospels were compiled and written down in the light of various faith communities' ongoing experience of the risen Christ. Father Brown takes this for granted, and it sometimes gives right-wing Catholics fits.

At the same time, he also insists that the Gospels are not fiction. They reflect theologically and communicate truth based on historical facts. This sometimes gives left-wing Catholics fits of their own. The joy of the intellectual life shines with particular brightness in the writings of a scholar such as Father Raymond Brown. You can't do better than this.

Joan Chittister, O.S.B.

A Benedictine and former prioress of a community of Benedictine nuns in Pennsylvania, Joan Chittister is one of the most articulate and on-the-money American Catholic intellectuals writing today. In *Wisdom Distilled from the Daily* (Harper & Row, 1990), Joan Chittister reflects on the meaning of the Rule of St. Benedict — upon which all Benedictine communities base their life — for an everyday spirituality in today's world. Discussing the Benedictine ideal of "stability," she writes:

> Commitment...is not necessarily our long suit these days. Nothing in this society requires it and everything militates against it. It is not expected, after all, to promise to stay at a thing when something bad happens to it or something seemingly better comes along. It is not easy to continue the hard work of being here when everything around us says go there where it will be easier. It is hard to go on when it would be so much simpler just to quit. But the question becomes, what will happen to me as a person if I don't go on, if I don't persevere, if I don't persist, if I don't see this through?
>
> In the first place, I will certainly fail to learn a great deal about myself if I leave a thing before it's finished. I will fail to learn the strengths that give me quality. And I will fail to face the weaknesses that call for change. I will end up being less than I can be....
>
> In the second place, I will lose the opportunity to grow. Stability is the quality that enables me to confront life's questions with both self-knowledge and self-giving. Not every question reveals itself at once. Not every effort succeeds at first attempt. Not every good thing that happens, happens without persistent purpose and continual failure.

We live in a world that believes in the easy out. If it starts to hurt the only answer is to run away. Joan Chittister's words apply to anything from marriage to a vocation that requires religious celibacy. Her words apply to anything that demands persistence and faithfulness, from finishing a college degree to cleaning out the garage. You said you would stay and stick with it. You promised. You made a permanent commitment. You'll get no encouragement from "the world," but in your heart you know what's right. You know.

For Catholicism, the intellectual life is basic to the life of faith. It's a basic source of knowledge, understanding, and joy. But it takes what the Rule of St. Benedict calls "stability," stick-to-it-iveness, discipline. Dedication. The will to shut off the television set, pick up a book, and read. That's the basic connection, and there is joy to be found therein. Joy that Catholicism has known about for centuries. Joy that is free to anyone willing to accept it.

Imagine that.

CHAPTER EIGHT

The Joy of
Catholic Institutions

Something there is in the modern spirit that does not like an institution. For many people today, institutions stand for rigidity, power structures, insensitivity, and pushy authoritarianism. Not so long ago, the term "institution" was synonymous with a place of confinement such as a prison or mental asylum. If you were "institutionalized" you could not function in society at large. Normal people were not in "institutions."

More specifically, today it is fashionable to look down one's nose at "institutional religion." It's socially acceptable to be religious or "have a spirituality" as long as it is a private, personal, eclectic, "noninstitutional" affair. If you accept an "institutional religion" and take its traditions, beliefs, and ideals seriously, you are a hopeless geek. It's okay if you were "raised Catholic," but it needs to be something in your past if you want to be "culturally correct." If you still consider yourself to be a member of the church and a "practicing Catholic," then you are beyond hope. Why hand over your personal freedom to an institution? Why allow your totally unique, open, ever so expansive spirituality to be confined by the doctrines and dogmas of a single "institutional religion"? Thus that witty bumper sticker: MY KARMA RAN OVER MY DOGMA.

But look. "Institution" is not a four-letter word. As we are using it here, the term simply means — to quote from a dictionary — "an established organization or foundation, especially one dedicated to public service or to culture." The term "institution" is neutral; it has no positive or negative connotations in itself. An institution can be either good or bad depending on its purpose. Simply because an institution exists does not make it worthy of scorn. Neither does an institution automatically deserve praise simply because it's an institution.

Here is the fact of the matter. Institutions are unavoidable. When two or more people join for a shared purpose, before long they become an institution with rules, however minimal. "We will meet on Thursdays at 7:30 p.m." Bingo, you have an institution. In fact, dear reader, the only alternative to institutions is anarchy, disorder, and confusion, everything going in all directions at once. Nothing would ever be accomplished without institutions.

Christianity had to become an institution called the Christian church if it was to survive and fulfill its purpose. It could not remain a freewheeling movement. Thus, within a few decades after the death and resurrection of Jesus, Christianity developed institutional leadership structures, "rules and regulations," doctrinal formulations, and so forth. It had to happen, and there is something thoroughly Catholic about this. Recall that for Catholicism "things" can both carry God's love and cause God's love to be present in the world and in human communities. "Things" can be sacramental.

In the current cultural climate here is a most eye-popping Catholic belief. Catholicism believes that even institutions can carry God's love and cause God's love to be present in the world. Even institutions. This is tough for the modern spirit to accept, a bitter pill. Doesn't "institutional religion" put you in a spiritual straitjacket? Make you do things you don't want to do? Force you to accept embarrassing beliefs? Tell you that you can't do whatever you feel like doing whenever you feel like doing it?

It all depends on what you mean by "freedom" and "liberty" and "happiness" and "love." If by freedom you mean being able to do whatever you feel like doing whenever you feel like doing it, yes, Catholicism has a different understanding of freedom.

If by liberty you mean an easy rider life free of all commitment and the constraints that come with it, yes, Catholicism has a different understanding of liberty.

If by happiness you mean the constant ability to satisfy any and all wishes and desires as soon as you have them regardless of the cost to anyone else, yes, Catholicism has a different understanding of happiness.

If by love you mean a feeling of emotional effervescence, yes, Catholicism has a different understanding of love, as well.

Precisely *because* it is an institution the Catholic Church can help people experience true freedom, liberty, happiness, and love. Right here. Right now.

This is a hard saying for the contemporary, with-it, nobody-tells-me-what-to-do attitude. Nobody tells this attitude what to do. Except movie, television, and rock 'n' roll celebrities, of course. This attitude thinks like celebrities seem to think and acts like celebrities seem to act because, well, celebrities are so, you know, *cool.* This attitude, in other words, is as adolescent as it can be. But it's the "in" attitude.

In some ways, we're a nation of adolescents, and we can't believe that an institution such as the Catholic Church could know the first thing about freedom, liberty, happiness, and love. No way. Television talk show hosts, television commercials, my own subjective point of view, they are the source of truth, not the church.

The Catholic Church is not only an institution, but its institutional character can be a source of unimaginable joy. Because it has a sacramental nature — because it carries God's love into the world and causes God's love to be present in the world — the Catholic Church as an institution constitutes a most reliable source of guidance and nourishment for those who seek authentic freedom, liberty, happiness, and love.

This is delightful news, it's true. But the Catholic Church is a human institution. That means it is not only gloriously good at what it does. It is also gloriously inept sometimes. Two left feet. Shoestrings tied together. Here and there, now and then.

In some ways some times, and in other ways other times, the Catholic Church as an institution hasn't a clue. It's true. But the institutional church is like an elderly aunt that everyone loves despite her eccentricities. She does so many things well, and is so basically good, well-meaning, and lovable, that we can overlook the things she doesn't do well. She sees things with such clarity most of the time that we can overlook the situations where she is shortsighted.

The Catholic Church is like the family as G. K. Chesterton described the family:

> Of course the family [substitute "the church"] is a good institution because it is uncongenial. It is wholesome precisely because it contains so many divergences and varieties. It is...like a little kingdom, and, like most other little kingdoms, is generally in a state of something resembling anarchy.... Aunt Elizabeth is unreasonable, like mankind. Papa is excitable, like mankind. Our youngest brother is mischievous, like mankind. Grandpapa is stupid, like the world; he is old, like the world.

Actually, within the institution we call the Roman Catholic Church there are a number of smaller institutions including the papacy, the curia — the Vatican bureaucracy, if you will — the college of cardinals, the bishops, the priests, dioceses, and parishes. There are religious orders and congregations. Each of these is an institution with its own unique characteristics and purposes.

Probably the most Catholic institution in many people's eyes is the papacy. People ask, rhetorically, "Is the pope Catholic?" This is because the papacy is probably the most visible Roman Catholic institution. No other Christian body has an institution to compare with this one. Indeed, the papacy is of basic importance to Catholicism.

Keep in mind, however, that the papacy has changed a great deal down through the centuries, and it is subject to still further change as time goes by. One of the most recent changes happened when Pope John Paul I, who died after being in office for only a month, in 1978 refused to be crowned as a kind of religious monarch using the traditional triple crown. He preferred, instead, to be simply "installed." His successor, John Paul II, followed his example. Thus, the papacy left behind a regal spirit inappropriate to the modern era and embraced a more pastoral image.

This is how it is: Catholicism believes that the pope, whoever he may be, is the successor of the apostle Peter. Peter was the first called by Jesus to follow him (Matt. 4:18, Mark 5:37), and he often served as a representative for the other disciples. Peter may have been the first disciple to whom the risen Christ appeared, at least that's the case in Luke's Gospel and the Acts of the Apostles and in the writings of Paul. In the Gospels of Matthew, Mark, and John, however, Mary Magdalene of the bad reputation is first to see the risen Lord.

Here are the classic biblical texts Catholicism refers to for its understanding of the central place of the pope as successor to Peter:

> Now when Jesus came into the district of Caesarea Philippi, he asked his disciples, "Who do people say that the Son of Man is?" And they said, "Some say John the Baptist, but others Elijah, and still others Jeremiah or one of the prophets." He said to them, "But who do you say that I am?"
>
> Simon Peter answered, "You are the Messiah, the Son of the living God." And Jesus answered him, "Blessed are you, Simon son of Jonah! For flesh and blood has not revealed this to you, but my Father in heaven. And I tell you, you are Peter, and on this rock I will build my church, and the gates of Hades will not prevail against it. I will give you the keys of the kingdom of heaven, and whatever you bind on earth will be bound in heaven, and whatever you loose on earth will be loosed in heaven." (Matt. 16:13–19)

> [Jesus said:] "Simon, Simon, listen! Satan has demanded to sift all of you like wheat, but I have prayed for you that your own faith may not fail; and you, when once you have turned back, strengthen your brothers." And he said to him, "Lord,

I am ready to go with you to prison and to death!" (Luke 22:31–32)

When they had finished breakfast, Jesus said to Simon Peter, "Simon son of John, do you love me more than these?" He said to him, "Yes, Lord; you know that I love you." Jesus said to him, "Feed my lambs." A second time he said to him, "Simon son of John, do you love me?" He said to him, "Yes, Lord; you know that I love you." Jesus said to him, "Tend my sheep." He said to him the third time, "Simon son of John, do you love me?" Peter felt hurt because he said to him the third time, "Do you love me?" And he said to him, "Lord, you know everything; you know that I love you." Jesus said to him, "Feed my sheep. Very truly, I tell you, when you were younger, you used to fasten your own belt and to go wherever you wished. But when you grow old, you will stretch out your hands, and someone else will fasten a belt around you and take you where you do not wish to go." (He said this to indicate the kind of death by which he would glorify God.) After this he said to him, "Follow me." (John 21:15–19)

Now, there is no getting around one fact. All four Gospels portray Peter as a world-class klutz who, all the same, had a good heart. Not too bright, but reliable in the long run. In Peter the papacy had humble beginnings, and perhaps it should be more humble in the future than at times in the past. In our own time, for sure, the church needs a pope who leads by his example of humility, joy, simplicity, and courage. We don't need a pope who tries to lead by scolding.

Since the late 1960s, popes have spoken out clearly about human rights, economic justice, war and peace, and other topics of deep concern to the modern world. However, these same popes have insisted on teachings about human sexual behavior — the prohibition of artificial methods of birth control being the best known — that place them at odds with countless millions of sincere, dedicated Catholics. Paradoxically, these teachings have had an eroding effect on the teaching authority of the pope. Instead of strengthening his role, they have weakened it. Which is sad.

This is the best example of ways in which recent popes have edged perilously close to projecting an aura of infallibility when infallibility is theologically and historically impossible. Any attempt to attach infallibility to the birth control teaching would plunge the church into a crisis from which it might not recover for a hundred years or more. But more about infallibility in a moment...

In such circumstances how can we speak of the papacy being a source of joy? For many, it is a matter of joy with a patina of sorrow. When Pope John Paul II visited the United States in 1993, for the World Youth Congress in Denver, Colorado, he received a wildly enthusiastic reception from thousands and thousands of young people. Without question, this was a joyful event. The young people experienced the pope as a powerful symbol of hope and life, even though when asked many said they could not agree with the official teaching on birth control and they thought women should be allowed to become priests. To rejoice in the pope does not require agreement with him on everything he says. The pope is only human, after all.

The papacy is always shaped by the personal theology and spirituality of the man who happens to be pope. A man with a grim or defensive outlook on life and the world will be a very different pope from one who is hopeful, joyful, and inspiring. Pope John XXIII was a man of joy and hope, and it showed in his papacy from 1958 until his death in 1963. He once said:

> In the everyday exercise of our pastoral ministry, greatly to our sorrow, we sometimes have to listen to those who although consumed with zeal do not have very much judgment or balance. To them the modern world is nothing but betrayal and ruination. They claim that this age is far worse than previous ages, and they go on as though they had learned nothing at all from history — and yet history is

the great teacher of life. . . . We feel bound to disagree with these prophets of misfortune who are forever forecasting calamity.

Pope John XXIII felt deeply about the need for the pope to lead not by stern commands or condemnations but by example and inspiration. Another time he said:

Today the Spouse of Christ [i.e., the teaching church] prefers to use the medicine of mercy rather than severity. She considers that she meets the needs of the present age by showing the validity of her teaching rather than condemnations.

Keeping in mind, then, that the papacy has great potential to lead by inspiring joy, courage, and hope — although a pope sometimes acts otherwise — let us turn our attention to basic principles. There is considerable theological ferment these days over the nature and purpose of the papacy, so we will confine ourselves to the two main Catholic doctrines that concern the papacy. Beyond this we will leave the debate to the experts.

The first doctrine says that the pope has "primacy" over the whole church. This does not mean that he runs an absolute monarchy. Hardly. It means that the pope is supposed to be a symbol of Christian unity. Ironically, the papacy is one of the biggest stumbling blocks to Christian unity, since Protestants have big problems with the papacy. But that's another topic. Since Pope John XXIII in the early 1960s, the popes have encouraged dialogue with other Christian traditions, which may one day lead to some form of genuine Christian unity. Which is a step in the right direction.

For Catholics, the pope is a source of joy because he constantly calls us back to the spirit of the Gospel, the Good News of God's love. The pope comforts and challenges us, just as the Gospel does. When we need to hear something, sometimes the pope says just what we need to hear. Sometimes he doesn't, of course. But that's another topic.

To say that the pope has "primacy" over the church does not mean that he can tell all Catholics what to do and they had better obey or else. Freedom of conscience is the Catholic bottom line, although it is important for us to have a conscience well informed by the Gospel, by prayer, by serious consideration of official church teachings, and by accurate information from other sources. (See the quotation from Pope John Paul II on p. 77 above.)

The second basic doctrine that relates to the papacy is the doctrine of papal infallibility, or immunity from error. Some people have a nutty idea. They think that Catholics believe that every time the pope says anything about anything he is immune from error. Unfortunately, sometimes popes themselves talk and act as if this is true. Someone has called this "creeping infallibility." But that's another topic. The truth is that a pope speaks infallibly only under some very strict conditions.

The pope speaks infallibly only when:

- he defines a doctrine of faith or morals speaking as the head of the church and with the definite intention of telling the whole church what's what;

- he is in the act of defining a dogma of faith, which means that there are many popes who were never infallible because they never did this;

- there is close cooperation between the pope and the bishops in the process of making an infallible statement, and the clear consensus of the people who constitute the church is in agreement.

So, let's have none of this "the pope is infallible all the time" nonsense. In fact, a pope has spoken infallibly only once since the doctrine of infallibility emerged from the First Vatican Council in 1870. In 1950, Pope Pius XII announced infallibly that the Blessed Virgin Mary was assumed, body and soul, into heaven. That's it. No pope before or since has spoken infallibly.

Popes make mistakes and have their blind spots. It's not the pope's job to make public the mind and will of God on every possible question. On many issues, the pope has no idea what God wants us to do. He's as much in the dark as everyone else, struggling to find the answer.

As much as some people may crave a pope who would be infallible and all-knowing all of the time, who would have all the answers to all our problems, such a craving is unfair, unrealistic, and a symptom of emotional and spiritual immaturity. It could also be a form of idol worship. The pope is not God, for Pete's sake. First and foremost, the pope is a fellow believer. Then he is the bishop of Rome and the pope, and he does the best he can.

Pope John Paul II said it well in *Crossing the Threshold of Hope*. First he quotes St. Augustine of Hippo: "I am a bishop for you, I am a Christian with you." Then he adds that "*christianus* [Christian] has far greater significance than *episcopus* [bishop], even if the subject is the Bishop of Rome."

As with so many other aspects of Catholicism, it is possible both to take the papacy too seriously and not seriously enough. In the nineteenth century some Catholics, called "ultramontanists," virtually *worshiped* the pope. Some called the pope "Vice-God of Mankind." Others called him "Permanent Word Incarnate." Today's spiritual descendants of the ultramontanists don't go that far, but they often act as if every time the pope speaks — especially if they agree with him — it's as good as God speaking. Risky business. On the other hand, some Catholics pay almost no attention to the pope, and in doing so they miss out on a vital source of spiritual guidance, inspiration, and wisdom.

The papacy is meant to be a source of joy, but it cannot be a source of genuine joy and spiritual liberation if we view it as a way to avoid the holy mystery of our own lives and the holy, absolutely transcendent mystery of God. The papacy isn't an answer machine; it's a source of hints — sometimes inspired hints, but hints all the same. Not even the pope has an absolute grasp on the mind of God. When the pope says something, that doesn't mean we can stop thinking about it because he — and so God —

has spoken. It means we need to *begin* thinking — and praying — about it, because the pope wouldn't bring it up if it wasn't important.

Indeed, whoever the pope may be at any given time, he has a unique role on the stage of the modern world. Not only Catholics pay attention to what he says and does, but other Christians take him seriously too. Even non-Christians look to the pope for leadership toward peace in the world and greater understanding and cooperation between all people. What a joy it is for Catholics to know that their pope is, in a very real sense, a spiritual leader for the whole world.

The papacy is perhaps the most visible Catholic institution, but it isn't the only one. The institution most Catholics come into contact with most often is their local parish. A parish is a geographical entity, taking in a certain piece of territory on the map. But that's about the only blanket statement you can make about all parishes. Parishes are as unique as the places they are located and the people who populate them.

There are old parishes, new parishes, city, suburban, and rural parishes, conservative parishes, liberal parishes, and middle-of-the-road parishes, affluent parishes and poor parishes, and a great many parishes that are neither. There are ethnic parishes — Irish, African American, Polish, Italian, Hispanic, German, and Vietnamese among the most common — and there are countless parishes that are a mix of many ethnic groups.

In parishes we discover the truth of something said years ago by the great twentieth-century Irish and more-or-less Catholic writer James Joyce. Describing the Catholic Church, he said: "Here comes everybody."

In a Catholic parish no matter which one you choose, you will find a motley crew. Heavy on the motley, as I said in an earlier chapter. Some people welcome you with open arms; others ignore you, at least until you "get involved." In a Catholic parish, humanity runs rampant. All over the place. There are irritating people, friendly people, reserved people, and people who gush. Catholics are human beings; it's as simple as that. They have their strengths and weaknesses; they have their virtues and foibles. Therefore, anyone patient enough to find a niche can find a place to fit in.

Once we leave the parish and venture into other church structures and institutions, things get confusing. Try to bear with me.

Between the parish and the Vatican is a geographical institution called a diocese. An especially large and important diocese is called an archdiocese. Each diocese encompasses many parishes, sometimes hundreds of them. Each diocese has a bishop in charge, and each archdiocese has an archbishop in charge. The distinction between a bishop and an archbishop is purely honorary, by the way.

Some archbishops are also cardinals, another honorary position except that cardinals under the age of eighty get to vote for a new pope when a pope dies. The "college of cardinals," which can number no more than 120 under the age of eighty, may also serve as a special advisory group to the pope.

Also, there are bishops, archbishops, and cardinals who receive their title more as an honor than anything else. A "titular bishop" has no diocese to run, usually because he works in the Vatican and became a bishop for honorary reasons. In some cases a titular bishop is one because he was appointed to run a diocese in a country where the government hates the church and won't allow him to take over his diocese. Persecution of Catholics and that sort of thing.

Some dioceses and archdioceses are so large the "ordinary" — the actual bishop in charge who generally is not ordinary at all — has assistant bishops called "auxiliary bishops." Now and then you see a "coadjutor bishop," which is a bishop appointed to help the main bishop, but in this case the helper bishop will become the main bishop when the present main bishop retires or buys the farm. Did you get all that?

You may ask, and with good reason I might add, "Where is the joy in all this?" Well, there is a certain quiet joy in the fact that, bureaucratic as it is, still all this business of dioceses and bishops and so forth adds up to a certain degree of order and stability. It's imperfect, yes, but by and large it works. In a frequently chaotic world that's one source of quiet joy.

But there is another perspective, too. If we step back and not take the whole thing too seriously we have to laugh. It really is hilarious the way the whole show lends itself to pretentiousness. One thinks of the title of Herb Gardner's wonderful play that became a movie in the mid-1960s, *A Thousand Clowns*. For all its serious, legitimate, and important functions, the church's structures and leadership roles can sometimes look like a three-ring circus. But, hey, who doesn't love a circus?

The church's institutions are human attempts to give some form and order to a divine undertaking, the proclamation and living of the Gospel of Jesus the Christ. The challenge to these institutions is to facilitate this undertaking. Sometimes, for all their good intentions, the institutions get in the way. Instead of opening doors they close doors.

Like the Gospel, the church's institutions are supposed to bring spiritual liberation and healing — "salvation" — into people's lives. Much of the time, they actually do this. They do it imperfectly, but they do it. It's important to give pats on the back where pats on the back are due. It's easy to be a cynic about church institutions, but cynicism is the easiest thing in the world. Sometimes it takes humility, courage, and love to embrace Catholicism in spite of its institutional faults and failings. In the long run it's worth it and the joy one discovers there is a joy that runs deep, a joy that is reliable.

There is a healthy attitude to have with regard to the church's institutions: they aren't perfect, but neither are we. The "institutional" church's doors are open to anyone. To paraphrase the great Protestant theologian Paul Tillich, there is great joy in accepting oneself as accepted — by the "institutional" church as well as by God — in spite of being unacceptable.

CHAPTER NINE

The Joy of the Ordinary

What is the ordinary after all? The word "ordinary" is related to the Latin *ordo*, which originally meant "a row of threads in a loom." The ordinary is a source of joy precisely because it is characterized by "everydayness." The ordinary is like a row of threads in a loom, a variety of colors, all in a row, all spaced evenly, nothing out of the...well, out of the *ordinary*. All the threads are where they belong, in a row, as the weaver works on the loom, weaving the threads into a garment, blanket, or rug, something beautiful and useful.

There is joy in the ordinary because it is so quiet and unassuming. In the ordinary there is nothing unusual, nothing extraordinarily good, but nothing extraordinarily bad, either. It is just...the ordinary, all the threads of our lives where they belong. In this ordinariness Catholicism finds joy because this is where the Divine Mystery is most hidden and most present.

Because there is nothing unusual in the ordinary, we find it difficult to find God there. But for Catholicism this is what makes the ordinary so utterly sacred. For the Son of God graced the ordinary by taking it for his own. He became an ordinary human being, except that he was "without sin" (Heb. 4:15). He gestated in the womb of a woman for nine months, in the ordinary way, and was born in the simplest of circumstances. He slipped into the world from between his mother's legs, in the ordinary way, most likely into the waiting hands and joyful heart of Joseph. Joseph, the man who would be the earthly/ordinary father to the

Son of God. Joseph, who would make it seem for Jesus perfectly
natural to call God his *Abba,* his loving Papa.

The Son of God had an ordinary infancy, sucking and pok-
ing gently at his mother's breasts, gulping contentedly the sweet
milk that flowed into his mouth. He gurgled and burped, cooed,
smiled, and cried in the night as babies always do. He crawled
on the ground and learned to walk by standing and falling and
standing again. First one step, then another, in the ordinary way.
Mary and Joseph helped the Son of God, as a tiny boy, learn to
control his bladder and bowels, in the ordinary way. The child
Jesus experienced childhood illnesses, he had fevers and chills, he
sneezed and had a runny nose and a sore throat. He begged for
things he couldn't have, as children do.

Anything that is a part of childhood and growing up, the Son
of God experienced for himself because it is ordinary, gloriously
ordinary. The Son of God had ordinary human sexuality and
the sexual hormones and feelings that surge during adolescence.
Adolescent erections and nocturnal "wet dreams" are ordinary for
boys, so Jesus had these experiences as well. If taking note of this
shocks or embarrasses us, then we don't really believe that the Son
of God became a complete human being. Just like us. Exactly
like us.

We have scriptural evidence that hints at the most ordinary of
early adolescent rebellions. The second chapter of Luke's Gospel
tells the famous story of the twelve-year-old Jesus who, without
his parents' permission, stays behind in Jerusalem after everyone
else departs for home. Only a day later do Mary and Joseph discover that Jesus is missing, and they return to find him trading
insights with the teachers in the Temple. They scold him. Doesn't
he know how worried they have been? And what do they get?
Smart-mouth adolescent back-talk, that's what they get. Here is
how the exchange goes in Luke's Gospel:

> When his parents saw him they were astonished; and his
> mother said to him, "Child, why have you treated us like
> this? Look, your father and I have been searching for you in

great anxiety." He said to them, "Why were you searching for me? Did you not know that I must be in my Father's house?" (Luke 2:48–49)

We gloss over the adolescent Jesus' words with a predictable piety, but it's just as easy to hear in his reply a smart-aleck tone of voice. Which seems more natural, more ordinary.

Jesus lived the most ordinary of lives, evidently, because after this scene in the Temple we learn nothing more about him until the beginning of his public ministry at about the age of thirty. In other words, the Son of God lived far longer in ordinary obscurity than he did in the public eye.

The ordinary is, therefore, nothing to look down upon. Nothing is holier than the ordinary. Because God created the ordinary, and because the Son of God became an ordinary human being in all things except sin, and because by his death and resurrection he redeemed the ordinary from its fallen condition, the ordinary, the everyday, is holy.

Here is an astonishing thing, an amazing thing, a thing to make you sit up and take notice. For Catholicism the ordinary is holy, and yet it remains so...ordinary. Perplexing! A puzzlement! We miss the holiness of the ordinary because the holy is so ordinary. Yes. We are surrounded by all things holy but because the holy is so ordinary we miss it most of the time. What are we to do?

We need sacred words to help us remember the holiness of the ordinary, to help us not forget about it. Words we can chant to help see the Divine Mystery all around us. Words that transcend past and future, wondrous words, words to awaken us to the holy all around us. But they can't be tired words, pious words. No, we need words to ring in our ears, to echo lightly in our heart. We need words to shake us out of our daily dose of grim, words that will open our eyes and sing in our ears....

How about words from a poem, "In No Strange Land," by Catholic poet Francis Thompson (1859–1907): "O world invisible, we view thee."

The ordinary days of our lives are soaked with the divine presence and they bring us divine presents, day in, day out. But so
rarely do we recognize what's happening, so earnestly do we go
about our daily tasks. Catholicism rings out the holiness in the
ordinary, and these words are as good as any to wake us up. Sing
them and snap your fingers: *O world invisible, we view thee.*

Of course, simply because we are in the ordinary, because all
the threads are where they belong, in a row, does not mean we
have our act together. All our threads in a row does not necessarily
mean we also have all our ducks in a row. Catholicism finds joy
in the ordinary even when the ordinary is unpredictable, when we
do not have our act together, when we do not have all our ducks
in a row.

The ordinary is holy because we are doing the best we can. We
do not have all our ducks in a row, but we're doing the best we
can. We do not have our act together, but we're doing the best we
can. The ordinary is frequently chaotic and unpredictable. The
threads in the loom are different colors and they get mixed up
sometimes, even much of the time. But the resulting garment,
blanket, or rug, is more interesting that way. When we're doing
the best we can.

Catholicism does not romanticize the ordinary. *O world invisible, we view thee.* Absolutely not. There is a wonderful line in
a delightful novel, *She's Come Undone,* by Wally Lamb (Pocket
Books, 1992). Proposing marriage, Thayer says to his girlfriend,
Dolores: "I ain't offering you happily-ever-after. I'm offering
you...happily-maybe-sometimes-ever-after. Sort of. You know,
with warts and shit." (You should pardon the indelicate word.)

This is the ordinary that Catholicism rejoices in, the ordinary punctuated regularly with hassles, inconvenience, and other
people who are a pain in the butt. This is the ordinary that is
holy, the ordinary the Son of God embraced with love. *O world
invisible, we view thee.* The joy Catholicism finds in the ordinary
is sometimes. Sort of. "With warts and shit." But joy all the same,
joy deeper than all the hassles, inconvenience, and people who are
both a pain in the butt and a grace in our life.

Listen to a question. How does Catholicism discover the holy in the ordinary? Like a kid who pushes her nose up against the plate glass window of an old-fashioned toy store. That's how. We're not talking Toys Backwards-R Us, here, mega-store city. For there is little if any joy in such a place, only big-time overload. On the contrary. We're talking Mr. Plumworthy's Toy Store down on Main Street, Smalltown, U.S.A. That's where the wonder is.

The plate glass window is the ordinary in our lives, the flat, smooth surface of the everyday ordinariness of our lives. Most of the time we walk right by the window. Especially if we're grownups. It's all so ordinary. But listen. We can stop. We can stop and press our nose up against the smooth surface of the glass and look, make a little steam ghost on the glass with our breath, and look to see what's on the other side in Mr. Plumworthy's display window. And then we see. Marvelous.

Whatever our work may be, here or there, it seems so ordinary. Even a brain surgeon's everyday work must get to be humdrum after a while. Ho hum, just another brain. Regardless, for most of us our work seems ordinary much of the time. Delivering this, working on that, repairing something else. Taking orders, selling, teaching other people's ordinary children. Ho hum. Playing the stock market, driving a bus, counseling, repairing computers, doing what lawyers do, ho hum. Whatever we do, ho hum.

Say we press our nose up against the smooth, cool surface of our everyday, ho hum work. Say we pause and do that. The Divine Mystery is on the other side of the glass. Catholicism finds joy on the other side of the ordinary. No matter how ordinary our work may seem, it puts us into contact with wonders. Press your nose up against the glass and look. Look.

First of all, we see that no matter what we are up to, our work involves us with other people. The people we work with. The people we work for. Therefore — and here is a great mystery of Christian faith and life — our work brings us into the presence of God. For God and people are not apples and oranges. Rather, God and people are six of one, half-dozen of the other. Push your nose up against the window, Catholicism says. To rub elbows with people is to rub elbows with God. *O world invisible, we view thee.*

The twentieth-century French philosopher Jean Paul Sartre had the opposite point of view, the old party pooper. He said (and I quote), *"L'enfer, c'est les autres."* Which means, loosely translated, "Other people are hell." Not a nice man at all. Well, he may have been nice enough personally, but this idea is grim and totally at odds with the joy of the ordinary. Catholicism says, No way. Other people are not hell. Other people are grace, and "grace" is just a word for God's own divine life. Grace is what other people are for us, and so they can bring joy. Do bring joy. Even when they are also a pain in the butt.

There is nothing more ordinary for most of us than other people, and sometimes other people can seem like hell on a bicycle. It's true. But when that's the case, others still bring us into contact with God who dwells in them and in our relationships with one another. Even irritating others are an occasion of grace. An opportunity to act in a loving manner.

Most of the time, of course, other people are congenial enough, easy enough to get along with. Most of the time the people we work with and for bring us the grace of the ordinary in pleasant enough ways. Most of the time. But we need, now and then, to remind ourselves of this. We need to press our nose up against the glass and look.

At the same time, work itself is ordinary. The tasks we carry out, the responsibilities we have, the job we must do, or the professional activities we stick with, all can seem so ordinary. But the work itself is a plate glass window. What is the work, after all, the ordinary work we do? Whatever our work may be, from frying up eggs and hash browns in a diner to teaching children how to read; from driving a long-distance truck to painting houses, you name it, the work is a way to be, be, be for others. It's a way to support ourselves, but at the same time, simultaneously, it is a way to help others have a life. In some way our work is a way to help other people have a life. And so, Catholicism says, there is joy to be had in your work. *O world invisible, we view thee.*

What is the work that you do? Press your nose up against the plate glass window of Mr. Plumworthy's store. Make a little ghost on the glass with your breath. Look inside at the marvelous display. What do you see? On the other side of the glass, on the other side of your work, there is God. The Divine Mystery. The Ground of All Being. Because your work is with and for others, there is joy.

Sometimes, of course, people forget that through faith we are meant to become "as a little child" (Mark 10:15). So they don't pause, now and then, to press their nose against the window to see what they will see there. Maybe they stand inches or feet away from the glass and look with little interest, but then the reflections in the glass obscure their view, reflections of sidewalk and street outside the shop. They forget what it is to be a child, to press their nose up against the glass to get a good look at what's inside. So they do not see clearly what their work is about, the vision on the other side, the wonderful vision of God who is there all the time.

When we press our nose up against the glass and keep it there for a minute, we see that our work is not only a way to see God, but our work is a way to bring the spirit of love — of peace, understanding, compassion, and forgiveness — into our little acre of the world. And so our work can be a source of joy. It is meant to be a source of joy.

Even more basic to our experience of the ordinary are our family relationships. There they are, those people we did not choose to have in our life. Holy moley. They come with the territory. Our parents, our children, our in-laws, cousins, aunts, uncles, and various hangers-on once or twice removed. Who knows where they came from? We're stuck with them, like it or not. Stuck like glue. We chose to marry the person we married, but his or her parents, siblings, and so forth — mostly so forth — all came to the party uninvited. We didn't select our parents and brothers and sisters either.

But let's not get ahead of ourselves. Let's begin at the beginning of any family network no matter how wild and crazy it may be. Prototypically, a family begins with a marriage. Hearts and flowers, romance, nibbling of the earlobes, goosey feelings and fireworks all lead to good old marriage. We choose our spouse amid a good deal of whoopie, and that's both wonderful and ordinary. It's not too difficult to see the joy in this particular ordinary, while the goosey feelings and fireworks last. Not too difficult at all. Funny thing about marriage, however. Eventually the love dust settles, the moon goes down, the sun comes up, and there is an ordinary day that needs to be lived. And another and another.... No goosey feelings, no fireworks. Ah, me. Time to intone the holy words: *O world invisible, we view thee.*

Marriage, any marriage, becomes ordinary. More or less ordinary. Catholicism takes a look at that, a quick look at that, and says: Fantastic! It's ordinary! Because, because a marriage is ordinary it is loaded with, you guessed it... God, the Divine Mystery, the Great Cosmic Wherewithal. And so marriage can be an endless source of joy, the joy of the ordinary. It's enough to drive wives and husbands into each other's arms again. And should. The nibbling of earlobes! Hearts and flowers and romance! The potential for joy in an ordinary marriage is just about endless. When you think about it. Because it is so ordinary.

Of course, most marriages lead to something else that is ordinary, spectacularly ordinary. Children. Parenthood. Life doesn't get more ordinary than this. A little nibbling of the earlobes, a giggle in the night, a squeaking of bedsprings, and the next thing you know, you're parents. The most innocent of pleasures leads to the most innocent-looking situation. Parenthood.

But it builds. Babies become toddlers, toddlers become children, children become teenagers, and then you're in for it. But time marches on — tramp, tramp, tramp — and, sweet Jesus, teenagers become young adults and no longer act like... ahem, well, like teenagers. They begin to act like human beings. More civilized that you ever dreamed possible. And somewhere down the line they're forty years old and you're old and getting older.

There is a great temptation for parents, at just about any time no matter the ages of their children, to sing with Littlechap in the Anthony Newley / Leslie Bricusse musical *Stop the World, I Want to Get Off!* There is a temptation to sing Littlechap's words and mean them: "For my little bit of pleasure I've been punished beyond measure." As soon as we sing the words, however, Catholicism replies: Hey. You. C'mon over here for just a sec. You there, with your face hanging out.

Nothing is more ordinary than having and raising children — conceived and delivered yourselves or adopted, it doesn't matter; kids are kids. Nothing is more ordinary, and nothing is more sacred. Parenthood is ordinary beyond words and a joy beyond words.

What do parents do? Besides tearing their hair out on a regular basis, I mean. No easy piety now. No trite phrases. Parents do exactly what the Jesus of the Gospels instructs his disciples to do. Press your nose against the plate glass window of Mr. Plumworthy's store. Parents die to self for the sake of their children. Parents forget themselves for the sake of their children. Parents lay down their lives for love of their children. Parents are like the grain of wheat that falls into the ground and "bears much fruit" (John 12:24). This is precisely what parents do. Precisely.

Parents can prove to you the paradox of the Gospel, that in the midst of all this ordinary death to self, all this ordinary forgetfulness of self, on the other side there is a new and deeper life, there is a special joy. This is not a cheap joy, not cheap at all. This joy has a price. For in the thick of it sometimes there is little light to see by. Sometimes there is deep anguish, tears, even wailing and gnashing of teeth. Parents sing a bluesy song sometimes: "Walkin' the floor over you." No cheap joy. But the joy comes, sooner or later the joy does come. No matter how much anguish a child may bring. And the joy is deep, deep beyond words to describe it.

Catholicism presses its nose up against Mr. Plumworthy's window and sees in ordinary parenthood the joy known only by those who say yes to the anguish true love often requires. In traditional Catholic language, they say yes to the cross and somewhere down the line comes resurrection, like a locomotive to knock them over.

That's what ordinary parenthood is like; ordinarily there is more sorrow and more joy than in just about any other human activity. Count on it.

So there is ordinary marriage and ordinary parenthood, and when we press our nose up against the window we see the joy at the heart of both. But there is another joy, another joy in an ordinary experience. It's the ordinary experience of family relationships of all kinds. What could be more ordinary than family life? Because family life is ordinary, Catholicism sees in it the presence of God's divine love.

Think about family life, any family's life. Your own, for example, no matter what shape it takes day in, day out. Think about it. What does your family look like? Who are the nudniks — one of which is you — who make up your family? Think about each one. Each one is special to you, even if each one is also a pest. Right? Or maybe — be honest, now — you like some of them better than others. Maybe you like some of them better at some times, others better at other times. That's the way it is when you live with nudniks. No need to apologize; it's the human condition. It's how we are. Time for the holy words to help us see the joy in the ordinary: *O world invisible, we view thee.*

Every family is knockabout. Families are more like whirling dervishes then calm collectives. Not here, not now. Maybe not anyplace ever. Family life is knockabout. Ordinarily so. Put two or three family members in the kitchen at the same time, at any time, and see what happens. Chances are they will not have a dream of an experience but a knockabout experience. Rough edges all over the place. Ordinarily. That's the way it is.

But it is precisely the ordinary knockabout experience of living in a family that is loaded with the potential for joy. Knockabout is joyful. Whirling dervish is joyful. Merely *being with* one's knockabout family carries a greater possibility for joy than anything else in life. That's what Catholicism says. We may think we crave the calm collective, but give us calm collective and after the novelty wears off we border on bonkers. Where's the action? What's happening around here? Where *is* everybody?

Sure, ordinary family life is ordinarily unpredictable. Trite but true: it has its ups and downs, downs and ups. Sometimes we moan and whine about the hassle of it all. But up and down the line, all things considered we'll take our ordinary family every time. Because that's where we are most likely to find rock-bottom joy.

There is one more thing to say about the joy Catholicism finds in the ordinary. Listen. Much of the time the joy we find in the ordinary is a joy that hides its face like a child and runs away laughing. What does this mean? The joy we find in the ordinary is ordinarily so rock bottom that we don't even know that it's there. Much of the time the joy that we feel is so deep within us as we work, as we go about a married merry-go-round, as we whirl in the whirlwind of our family, that we are not aware that the joy is even there. Imagine that.

Think about it honestly, you bundle of joy. You know that's what you are; you know that you are, don't deny it. You are a bundle of joy. Stop taking it for granted. You are breathing in and out, which is the most ordinary and most joyful thing in the world.

Catholicism says that you are a bundle of joy. But you are also thick-headed. So most of the time you are not aware that you are a bundle of joy. Think about it. Ponder the fact. *You are alive!* You are a bundle of joy. Regardless of what else goes on for you right now, you are a bundle of joy.

So you have your bummers. We all have our bummers. What might your current bummer be? Let's see. You could be unemployed. Bummer. But you are alive and, Catholicism whispers, God — the Divine Mystery — dwells in you. Don't just sit there. You are alive. Take a deep breath. The world is not ending. Ask for some help. Get with it. A job is just a job; a job is not your life. You will find another job. Take joy.

You could be depressed for whatever reason. Please, get some help. Talk to somebody about it. Don't sit in your own misery stewing like a potato. Do something. You are alive, are you not? You can act. You can. You are a bundle of joy. Take joy.

Maybe your marriage is a bummer, big time or little time. Come on. All marriages get to be bummers from time to time, now and then. It's no reason to give up. Talk to someone about it, someone who can do more than sympathize. Sympathy is nice, but in the long run it doesn't cut the mustard. Talk to someone who can offer practical advice. Read a book about marriage, a book based on more than psychology, a book on marriage with some spirituality to it as well. Make some effort to be more romantic, more erotic, more passionate. It's not all up to you, you know. You make a little bitty effort, God makes a great big effort. Catholicism says there is joy in ordinary marriage, but you have to make time to feel the joy. It does not happen by itself.

Sometimes we have pseudo-bummers. Bummers somebody else talked us into having, more or less. You can identify these when you hear people talk like this: "If only I could relax and just live my life with joy. If only I could get over my compulsions. If only I could get rid of my neuroses. If only I could find my inner child. If only I could just be myself."

What's the old Valley Girl phrase? "Gag me with a spoon." Behold the pseudo-bummer. Nobody grows up with a perfectly intact, totally healthy little psyche. So what? "Do some work," as they say, with a shrink or counselor. But get it over with as fast as possible, and get on with your life. Find a counselor who insists that either you finish your work in x number of sessions or you can go find somebody else to fritter away your time with. Which is what you would be doing after x number of sessions anyway.

You got bummers, I got bummers, all God's children got bummers. But big bummer or little bummer, regardless of the bummer in your life, remember, you are a bundle of joy. You are a bundle of joy, and life is waiting for you to get off your butt. Life sits on the curb out front waiting for you to come out and play. Don't keep life waiting or it may find someone else to play with. It's only temporary, you know. Life. Catholicism says: Find joy in your ordinary life, the life you have, not the life you wish you had.

Sing it. Snap your fingers: *O world invisible, we view thee.*

CHAPTER TEN

The Joy of Tradition

Every time it turns around, Catholicism finds joy someplace else, yet another source of joy. The foundation of it all, however, is the joy Catholicism finds in tradition. More accurately, Catholicism finds joy in Tradition (upper case "T") and traditions (lower case "t"). One and the other, both together.

Catholicism finds joy in traditions. Think back. Remember the first time you watched a live stage production or the movie version of the Joseph Stein / Jerry Bock / Sheldon Harnick musical *Fiddler on the Roof*? You don't have to be Jewish for the story and the music to touch your heart. You don't have to be Jewish because the story is universal; it speaks to human and spiritual needs we all have.

In fact, Catholics may be in a better position to find joy in *Fiddler on the Roof* than others because of our close kinship to Judaism. To quote Pope John Paul II, we think of the Jewish people as our "elder brothers and sisters." Catholics have a built-in radar, as it were, for customs and traditions that surface the sacred in the everyday.

Tevye, the poor Jewish milkman, explains the life his people live in the little village of Anatevka. The people of Anatevka keep their balance by maintaining their traditions. Everyone knows what the mamas do and what the papas do, what the sons and daughters do. Tevye explains about the local matchmaker, the village beggar, and "most important of all," the rabbi. He explains why the men keep their heads covered at all times and wear a little prayer shawl: "To show our constant devotion to God."

No one knows why the Jewish community of Anatevka does these things, but they all add up to...tradition. "Tradition!" Tevye and the chorus sing with joy. Tevye exclaims: "Without our traditions our life would be as shaky as...a fiddler on the roof!"

We envy Tevye, his wife, Golda, and their five daughters. We envy the people of Anatevka. They have something we do not. They have traditions that enable them to keep their balance. North American Catholicism had something of a unique subculture up until the early 1960s, but nothing to compare with the Jewish culture of Anatevka. All the same, there is a Catholic network of traditions and customs that, in their own way, help us to keep our balance by helping us to stay in touch with the holy in the everyday. Some of these are ethnic in origin, but many are shared by virtually all ethnic Catholic groups in one form or another.

We must take a little side trip into some important information. Bear with me. This is information that can sing in your heart. As with Judaism, Catholic traditions don't pop into existence out of nowhere. All customs and traditions are rooted in, express, and nourish Tradition. Tradition is the living source from which Catholicism draws its very existence. Look at any expression or manifestation of the Catholic faith you can find — including Scripture, liturgy, art, devotions, architecture, music, literature, poetry, theology, and philosophy — and you can trace it to Catholicism's nearly two-thousand-year-long experience of its living Tradition.

Tradition is the holy and hidden heart of the matter. "Tradition" is shorthand for the experience Catholic people have had for nearly two thousand years now, the experience of the real but hidden presence of the risen Christ. Or you could put it this way: Tradition is the faith as it is lived by the people who call themselves Catholic.

Tradition is *the* Catholic mystery because it is our human experience of faith, which is a living daily communion with the risen

Christ in our midst. Catholic traditions and customs, on the other hand, are ways to put into action or express faith. In his reference work *Catholicism* (HarperSanFrancisco, new edition, 1994), theologian Father Richard McBrien explains the relationship between Tradition and traditions thus:

> If a tradition cannot be rejected or lost without essential distortion of the Gospel, it is part of Tradition itself. If a tradition is not essential (i.e., if it does not appear, for example, in the New Testament, or if it is not clearly taught as essential to Christian faith), then it is subject to change or even to elimination. It is not part of the Tradition of the Church.

Tradition has been in existence from the beginning of the Christian faith, even before the New Testament. In fact, Tradition gave birth to the New Testament. It existed before and during the writing of the New Testament, and it continues to be the deep well from which we have drawn living waters during the many centuries since the New Testament was completed. This is why Catholics believe that while we can't do without the New Testament, the New Testament cannot be separated from or consulted apart from Tradition. To separate the New Testament from Tradition is to cut it off from its living origin and source.

This is delicate territory, so step lightly. There is always a subtle temptation to mistake traditions for Tradition. As Father McBrien explains, conservative Catholics sometimes confuse a nonessential custom or tradition — mandatory celibacy for priests, for example — with Tradition itself. For their part, liberal Catholics sometimes pooh-pooh something essential to Catholic faith — the Real Presence of the risen Christ in the Eucharist, for example — as if it were unimportant, even dispensable.

"The process of sorting out Tradition and traditions is ongoing," Father McBrien says, "and involves the official teaching authority of the Church, the scholarly authority of theologians, and the lived experience and wisdom of the Christian community itself."

All of this constitutes the theological nitty-gritty. Now back to our main stream, the celebration of joy that Catholicism finds in Tradition and traditions. This is a wonderfully rich and varied land that we hike into now. A regular kaleidoscope of spiritual riches. We can't discuss everything, but we'll touch on some of the main kinds of Catholic traditions and customs.

If Catholicism is known for anything it is known for its devotion to Mary. We relate to Mary as the mother of the Son of God. Thus, the early church honored Mary with the title "Mother of God" (Greek, *theotokos*). If Jesus was both fully divine and fully human, this title is not only appropriate but unavoidable.

The joy Catholicism finds in its devotion to Mary is part of Tradition. If this devotion were lost something essential would be lost as well, namely, the conviction that Jesus was both fully divine and fully human, Son of God and son of Mary. The forms this devotion takes, however, are traditions and customs, and they are numerous. Put on your seven-league boots and travel to just about any country or culture in the world and you will find unique local forms of devotion to Mary.

Even in our own time, there is widespread misunderstanding and misrepresentation of Catholicism's devotion to Mary. This is particularly true among evangelical Protestants. In a collection of essays entitled *Roman Catholicism* (John Armstrong, gen. ed., Moody Press, 1995), thirteen evangelical scholars and writers discuss their understandings of Catholicism. S. Lewis Johnson, Jr., author of an essay on Mary, betrays the classic evangelical Protestant misunderstanding of the place of Mary in Roman Catholicism. He writes:

> The gospel, as understood by the Reformers — by Luther, Calvin, and others — is not that propounded by the Church of Rome. In the one, there is the atoning Cross and one Mediator, the man Christ Jesus (1 Tim. 2:5); in the other, there is the Cross but two mediators, the man Christ Jesus and the woman, the Virgin Mary.

Professor Johnson's statement is preposterous. Roman Catholicism never has and never will believe that Mary, the mother of Jesus, has equal status and equal importance with Jesus. At the same time, however, we accord Mary a special place among the saints as the one chosen by God to be the mother of His Son.

Unfortunately, Professor Johnson could find plenty of evidence in certain popular Catholic writings and Marian piety to support his contention that Catholics accord Mary equal status with Jesus. Some Catholics go overboard when it comes to Mary. Sad to say. So it goes. When such Catholics do this, they might as well pin a sign to the backs of their shirts that reads "kick me," stroll up to some evangelical Protestants, turn around and bend over.

If you stick to the official doctrines of the church you will find no such extreme beliefs. Anything you find in the church's doctrines about Mary must be understood in the sense that she has a special place as the mother of Jesus. Even the most objective observer would have to say that this is appropriate. At the same time, Mary is subservient to Christ and serves his purposes as one of God's creatures. Mary can pray for us. Period.

In addition to her special role as the mother of the Messiah, however, Catholicism finds joy in Mary as a model for the rest of us. She is a model of faith — indeed, a model for what all of us, the church, are called to be, faithful carriers of Christ in the world.

Sometimes you will hear or read that Catholics "worship" Mary. This is flapdoodle. God alone is worthy of worship. Catholicism finds joy in the *veneration* of Mary — loving respect and devotion to her. We pray *to* Mary only in the sense that we ask her to pray *for* us. The most famous Marian prayer is half taken from the words of the angel to Mary in the Gospel of Luke, half a request for her prayers on our behalf:

> Hail Mary, full of grace, the Lord is with thee. Blessed art thou among women, and blessed is the fruit of thy womb, Jesus. Holy Mary, Mother of God, pray for us sinners now and at the hour of our death. Amen.

Parenthetically: Some Catholics today think that all use of archaic words in prayers, such as "thee," "thy," and "thou," should be done away with. Personally, I think there is room to retain some of these old words as appropriate for prayerful purposes. They carry meanings as poetry carries meanings, implications, and inferences that the pedestrian vernacular equivalents do not. In other words, what we have here is a little disagreement about a tradition....

Related to the basic Catholic devotion to Mary are devotions to her in the context of various "apparitions" or appearances she may have made. Thus, she is venerated with the titles Our Lady of Guadalupe (Latin America), Our Lady of Fatima (Portugal), and Our Lady of Lourdes (France). In recent years, there have been various purported Marian appearances, probably the most popular at Medjugorje, in the former Yugoslavia, but these have yet to receive official church acceptance or approval. In fact, the local bishop in Medjugorje refused to give the "appearances" any credence whatsoever.

When it comes to apparitions, Catholics are free to accept or reject because they are nonessential in the extreme. The "messages" supposedly announced by Mary at such events add nothing to what we already know from Scripture and Tradition. Nothing. Typically, "messages" from Mary are simply variations on the basic Gospel call to repentance and prayer.

Now and then a religious hysteric announces being on the receiving end of Marian appearances and messages. Such people are cracked nuts and should be ignored. They bring no joy. Often, the "messages" they say come from Mary are messages of gloom, doom, and impending disaster, which is not what the Gospel is about. Catholics who pay attention to such pitiful wackos gain no joy. All they do is lead non-Catholics to think that Catholics do not play with a full deck.

Devotion to Mary finds its most popular form in the Rosary. The Rosary is a form of devotional prayer. To pray the Rosary, typically you pray five sets of ten Hail Marys, each prefaced by an Our Father and concluded with a little prayer that begins, "Glory

be to the Father, and to the Son, and to the Holy Spirit…"
The Rosary begins with the Apostles' Creed, one Our Father,
three Hail Marys, and one Glory Be, and concludes with a longer
prayer to Mary, often "Hail, Holy Queen."

Each of the five "decades" of the Rosary is based on a "mystery," an event in the life of Jesus and/or Mary. The idea is to
let the meaning of the "mystery" sink in while praying. Scriptural
forms of the Rosary include brief readings from the Scriptures at
the beginning of each decade. The beads we use to keep track of
the prayers of the Rosary are "a rosary."

The Rosary isn't as complicated as it may sound, and it has
enjoyed phenomenal popularity for centuries. This may be because the Rosary is a physical form of prayer. By using beads to
count the prayers, we involve ourselves physically in the prayer
process. The beads give us something to hang on to, and in this
life sometimes we *need* something to hang on to.

There is joy in a traditional devotion such as the Rosary. Why?
Who can say? There is warmth and comfort in having the mother
of Jesus as a spiritual companion in prayer and as a companion on
our pilgrimage through time and space. It's a Catholic "thing,"
you might say. Either it grabs you or it doesn't.

Most Catholics pray the Rosary at one time or another, now
and then, here and there, but there are sincere Catholics who
never or hardly ever pray the Rosary. It's not required. It's
a tradition, a custom. Take it or leave it. But if you are a
Catholic, regardless of whether you like the Rosary or not,
chances are when you die your body will be buried with a rosary
wrapped around your hands. Some things Catholic you can't get
away from.

Actually, we need to look at the bigger picture here. Step back
for a wider view. We can't understand devotion to Mary unless
we understand the tradition of devotion to the saints in general.
Saints populate the Catholic landscape, and Catholicism has a
devotion to saints in general. By "saints" we mean people who
lived and died, and now they enjoy that better life we call, for
lack of a better word, "eternal." They occupy the eternal realm,

whatever that is, and they live better than we do. By a long shot. Catholicism believes that we can go on relating to these people who passed over the Great Divide. Also, we can ask them to pray for us just as we pray for one another Here Below.

This is part of Tradition. It's called the communion of saints, and we discussed it in chapter 4. If we don't believe in this we don't believe in eternal life, whatever it may be. If we don't believe in the communion of saints, we don't believe in heaven — whatever it may be. Not only that. The communion of saints includes not only personages of great holiness who are officially named as guaranteed saints ("canonized"). The communion of saints includes relatives and friends who died and go on living eternally. Whatever that may mean. We can go on relating to these people after they die. It's that simple. And they can pray for us. It's that simple. Imagine that.

It comes down to the conviction that our ultimate destiny does not lie in this knockabout world. Rather, we are created and destined for Something Better. We call it eternal life, but "eternal" isn't the same as "endless time"; it's Something Else. We know not what, except that it is a more complete intimacy with the love of God. Catholicism finds joy in the conviction — based on human faith experience — that we are made for relationships with one another and with God, and those relationships take a new and better form after we buy the farm.

The Catholic devotion to saints may mean continuing to relate to family and friends who have died. More than 40 percent of the population of the United States, according to empirical data, has had some form of comforting or inspiring encounter with the "presence" of a deceased loved one. Devotion to saints may also take the form of being in relationship with persons officially canonized by the church. Some of the best known are St. Francis of Assisi, St. Anthony of Padua, St. Jude, St. Teresa of Avila, St. Thérèse of Lisieux, and St. John of the Cross. But there are hundreds of others. It's like a big club that transcends time and space.

The bottom line, as with so many Catholic traditions, is that no one is required to have a devotion to saints. If it doesn't grab you, skip it. Devotion to the saints goes way, way back, to the days of the earliest Christians who asked their martyred fellow believers to pray for them when they gathered for liturgical celebrations. Most Catholics find joy in some form of devotion to saints. But skip it if you want to.

Closely related to the joy Catholicism takes in the Virgin Mary and the other saints is the tradition of setting up statues in our churches. Quite often older Catholic churches are decorated with more than a few statues of Jesus, Mary, various saints, and angels. This sometimes leads non-Catholics to charge Catholics with "idol worship," a charge that would be laughable were those who make it not so grimly serious.

Here is why Catholics have statues in their churches and take joy in statues. Each statue is there to remind us of a story. Far from worshiping the statue — a monumentally silly idea — Catholics see a statue and think of a story that encourages and inspires. Catholicism is a religion of stories, starting with the Gospels themselves. It's a tradition. Some of the stories are historically verifiable, others are legends, but both can carry truth and nourish faith.

Take one of the more common statues, which portrays St. Anthony of Padua holding the Christ Child in his arms. Here is the story in brief: Anthony, an Italian Franciscan friar during the early thirteenth century, was a guest in someone's home. A passerby saw him through an open window, deep in prayer. Anthony held Christ so intently in his heart that the observer saw the Christ Child in Anthony's arms. St. Anthony is the only person other than Mary, Joseph, and Simeon (Luke 2:27–29) to have had this privilege.

Statues of the crucified Christ, called crucifixes, remind us of Christ's love for us to the point of death. To meditate on a crucifix is to remember the Gospel accounts of Jesus' suffering and death. Indeed, all forms of statuary were originally story-telling devices, visual aids, if you will. The same goes for the images in stained-glass windows.

Another famous story is about St. Lawrence. According to the story — which may include legendary elements — on August 10, 258, the deacon Lawrence was tied by his persecutors to a flat framework of parallel metal bars and placed over a fire. Lawrence asked to be turned over when "the first side was done." As it happens, each year on the three nights following this anniversary the early morning sky is filled with a spectacular shower of meteorites. During the Middle Ages, people saw these "falling stars" at the rate of more than one every minute and called them "the tears of St. Lawrence" sparkling in the sky, shed from heaven over the cruelty of humankind.

Statues are important enough as a tradition, even today, that even in the newest Catholic churches you will find two or three simple statues placed in appropriate places. At the very least, these will include statues of Mary and Joseph, and perhaps a statue of the saint for whom the particular church is named. Behind every statue there is a story.

Catholics find joy in many stories that are purely fictional and have no statues to go with them. They are pure legend, but they have a charm of their own, all the same, for adults and children alike. One example is the story of why the robin's breast is red:

One morning, the sixth-century Irish saint Columba awoke in his little hermitage. He saw a robin perched on his window sill. "Do you have a song for me?" Columba asked. In response, the robin sang a song about Good Friday and how its breast got to be red. Here is the story:

From its nest, the robin saw the Lord upon the cross, and the Lord saw the brown, yellow-beaked bird. Jesus called to the robin, who flew and lighted upon his shoulder. The crowds taunted, and the robin sang, "Holy, holy, holy," its breast all the while against Jesus' bloody brow. Standing near the cross was Mary, and she spoke: "Christ's own bird thou shalt be!" So ever since then, the robin's proudest claim is that its red breast came from the day it saw Christ die upon the cross.

Catholic traditions and customs are almost countless. In his *Catholic Source Book* (Brown Roa Publishing Media, 1990), Rev.

Peter Klein divides them into nine categories: traditional prayers, scriptural traditions and customs, church traditions and customs, liturgical traditions and customs, devotions directed to God, devotions directed to saints and heroes, Catholic symbols, traditional words and phrases, and a general catch-all category for the odd custom or tradition that doesn't fit into any of the other categories.

Obviously, we can't discuss them all here. The important thing to remember is that Catholicism finds joy in traditions and customs because whatever they may be they are ways to cultivate faith. That there are so many Catholic traditions and customs is a tribute to the Catholic "feel" for God's presence in all kinds of situations and circumstances. In other words, for Catholicism God is always at home in the world, no matter when, no matter where.

One Catholic tradition belongs here, however, before we conclude our look at the joy of being Catholic. That is the tradition of lighting candles. Catholics light candles for many reasons and in many situations. We light candles during the Eucharist and other liturgical and paraliturgical celebrations. We give a lighted candle to a newly baptized person. We set up a huge lighted candle, called "the Paschal Candle," in the sanctuary of our churches on Easter. We light votive candles in little red glass cups as a sign of faith and prayer. In all cases, we light candles to remind ourselves of three things: that Christ is "the light of the world" (John 8:12 and 9:5), that we ourselves are to be "the light of the world" (Matt. 5:14), and that faith itself is a light to live by (Acts 26:18).

It's a joy to be Catholic, but this joy is not an end in itself. Rather, the experience of joy leads to actions for which the lighting of a candle serves as a metaphor. Because Catholicism knows a special joy, it responds by lighting candles of all kinds whenever possible — the lighted candles of active love for God and neighbor.

This is what Catholicism is about. And so there is joy.